The Whole Person

The Whole Person

Embodying Teaching and Learning through Lectio *and* Visio Divina

Edited by
Jane E. Dalton, Maureen P. Hall,
and Catherine E. Hoyser

ROWMAN & LITTLEFIELD
Lanham • Boulder • New York • London

Published by Rowman & Littlefield
An imprint of The Rowman & Littlefield Publishing Group, Inc.
4501 Forbes Boulevard, Suite 200, Lanham, Maryland 20706
www.rowman.com

6 Tinworth Street, London SE11 5AL

Copyright © 2019 by Jane E. Dalton, Maureen P. Hall, and Catherine E. Hoyser

Cover image: Mixed media collage, courtesy of Jane E. Dalton

All rights reserved. No part of this book may be reproduced in any form or by any electronic or mechanical means, including information storage and retrieval systems, without written permission from the publisher, except by a reviewer who may quote passages in a review.

British Library Cataloguing in Publication Information Available

Library of Congress Cataloging-in-Publication Data

ISBN: 978-1-4758-5148-9 (cloth)
ISBN: 978-1-4758-5149-6 (pbk.)
ISBN: 978-1-4758-5150-2 (electronic)

Contents

Foreword: Dining with the Imaginal Slowing Technologies of *Lectio Divina* and *Visio Divina*   vii

Acknowledgments   xi

Introduction   xiii

1   An Ancient Monastic Practice: Reviving It for a Modern World   1
   Jane E. Dalton, University of North Carolina at Charlotte; Maureen P. Hall, University of Massachusetts Dartmouth; Catherine E. Hoyser, University of Saint Joseph; Libby Falk Jones, Berea College

2   Embodying Deep Reading: Mapping Life Experiences through *Lectio Divina*   11
   Maureen P. Hall, University of Massachusetts Dartmouth

3   Image and Text: Toward Inner and Outer Wholeness   23
   Jane E. Dalton, University of North Carolina at Charlotte

4   *Lectio Divina* and Story-to-Poem Conversion as Tools for Transformative Education   37
   Catherine E. Hoyser, University of Saint Joseph

5   Reading the Word, the Self, the World: *Lectio* and *Visio Divina* as a Gateway to Intellectual and Personal Growth   49
   Libby Falk Jones, Berea College

6   Writing about Yoga: *Lectio Divina* and the Awakening of the Soul   61
   Mary Keator, Westfield State University

7 *Lectio Divina* as Contemplative, Anti-Oppressive Pedagogy in
   Social Justice Education Courses 71
   Elizabeth Hope Dorman, Fort Lewis College
8 Embodied Justice: We Are the Divine Text 87
   Vajra M. Watson, University of California, Davis
9 The Restorative Power of *Lectio Divina* and the Arts for
   University Lecturers 99
   Daphne Loads, University of Edinburgh

Appendix A: John Keats's poem "To Autumn" 111

Index 113

About the Editors 119

About the Contributors 121

Foreword

*Dining with the Imaginal
Slowing Technologies
of* Lectio Divina *and* Visio Divina

While food shopping recently I observed yet again the proliferation of convenient, even faster fast foods like dehydrated jerky and protein bars. This common fad nutrition seems to be necessary for eating on the run while navigating our busy lives. For the record, I have nothing against these products, only a curiosity about how overly salted, dried-out foods serve as an apt representation of trends that mirror our mind-numbing busyness.

It is the same with reading material as with quick food—under certain conditions, we carelessly digest information while hurrying from place to place. As opposed to our embrace of multitasking behavior or rushing toward red lights while driving, the slowing technologies of *lectio divina* and *visio divina* help us downshift and appreciate the content of soul-informing meditative practices (McDonald, 2012; Utterback, 2011). Waiting for us when we trade speed for unhurried, disciplined receptivity is the cascading poetry of inner awareness becoming felt, and eventually, articulated embodied experience.

When viewing a painting or reading an enlivened text, if we slow down, it can feel like a full-bloom experience of dining or even feasting on the work. Contemplative methods like *lectio divina* and *visio divina* support this goal of nurturing introspection so cherished by contemplative educators like Jane E. Dalton, Maureen P. Hall, and Catherine E. Hoyser. Together, they have assembled a group of inspiring authors to create *The Whole Person: Embodying Teaching and Learning through* Lectio *and* Visio Divina. Although the subject of this book originates from a Benedictine approach to reading scriptural texts, the integrity of the method can be secularized and made available to those who do not have ecumenical affiliations.

The process of *lectio divina* unfolds in four progressive steps, yet, like many contemplative practices, it spirals in helixes of personal revelation. The word *contemplation* is etymologically related to temple, *con-tem-plum,* and *contemplari*, which means to gaze with full attention (Mahony, 1998, p. 57). This sort of keen observation reveals numinous relationships that can emerge anywhere at any time, as in feeling into sacred texts, poetry, paintings, or the impact of an unforgettable landscape. As we mindfully enter these relationships, empathic attunement with the material acutely unfolds.

Beginning with reading, the power of the words kindles thoughts while leading to deeper understanding of the truth residing in the text (Merton, 2015). Language has the inventive power to conjure images that inspire the reader to find meaning in silence, sounds, and words (Dyczkowski, 1987). Openly receiving content then leads to meditative receptivity or what could be described as imaginal mindfulness. As I explored in my research on art as contemplative practice, this is when the reader nonjudgmentally observes and becomes absorbed in the moment-to-moment unfolding of emergent imagery (Franklin, 2016, 2017). Carefully observing the intelligent movements of internalized, text-based images eventually initiates sensations of amplified prayer. Abiding in the calm made available through reflective inquiry fills out this stage of the *lectio* practice.

To me it is important to add a fifth step to *lectio divina*, that of merging the wisdom gleaned from the practice into daily life (Merton, 2015). Living and applying the lessons received from the four stages is vitally important, since insight is rarely enough to effect trait changes beyond any contemplative practice. Direct day-to-day application of the surfaced wisdom is essential for anchoring our contemplative connections. Wisdom applied and lived is different from wisdom realized yet ignored.

DARSHAN AND *VISIO DIVINA*

Visio divina is similar to the Hindu yoga practice of darshan, or seeing the divine. Darshan, defined as "auspicious sight," focuses on revelations made available through theophanic vision (Eck, 1998, p. 3; Franklin, 2017, p. 74). *Visio divina* and darshan both result in beholding the divine around us while experiencing ourselves as the sacred same.

By observing the spiral-like phases of *visio divina* and *lectio divina*, students and teachers consciously modulate body-mind habits, judgments, and compulsions and welcome the introspective instincts of first-person and third-person voice. Said another way, subjectifying objective experience while objectifying subjective knowing connects together these recursive dimensions of interiorized life (Langer, 1951).

As I conclude this foreword, and to stay with the earlier theme, I am remembering a grocery store from my neighborhood growing up in the 1970s that was sold, gutted, and turned into a warehouse for artificial flowers. Then, as now, I saw a connection to embrace convenient, ersatz forms of beauty as aesthetic food. Similarly, traditional education and learning are often experienced as lifeless and barren, void of irrigating excitement. This carefully constructed book will help students and teachers trade the urge to catalog and memorize information, which is the stereotype of standardized learning and testing, for deeper passageways toward scholarship and knowing (Utterback, 2011). The question is, how do we continue to irrigate lifeless learning in order to dine with our emergent wisdom? Answers to this fundamental question will be found in the inspiring chapters that follow.

Michael A. Franklin, PhD, ATR-BC
Professor and Chair of the Graduate Art Therapy Program
Naropa University, Boulder, Colorado

REFERENCES

Dyczkowski, M. S. G. (1987). *The doctrine of vibration: An analysis of the doctrines and practices of Kashmir Shaivism*. Albany: State University of New York Press.

Eck, D. L. (1998). *Darsan: Seeing the divine image in India*. New York: Columbia University Press.

Franklin M. A. (2016). Imaginal mindfulness—imaginal intelligence: Musings on the languages of shadow and light in art, meditation, and clinical practice. In F. J. Kaklauskas, C. J. Clements, D. Hocoy, and L. Hoffman (Eds.), *Shadows & light: Theory, research, and practice in transpersonal psychology* (Vol. 1: Principles & Practices; pp. 101–21). Colorado Springs, CO: University Professors Press.

Franklin, M. A. (2017). *Art as contemplative practice: Expressive pathways to the SELF*. Albany: State University of New York Press.

Langer, S. (1951). *Philosophy in new key: A study in the symbolism of reason, rite, and art*. New York: New American Library.

Mahony, W. K. (1998). The artist as yogi, the yogi as artist. *Darshan: In the Company of Saints, 138*, 56–62.

McDonald, M. M. (2012). The soul-rich monk/priest: Thomas Merton on Lectio Divina. *Merton Annual, 25*, 197–204. Retrieved from http://search.ebscohost.com.naropa.idm.oclc.org/login.aspx?direct=true&db=aph&AN=97329807&site=ehost-live

Merton, T. (2015). Lectio Divina. *Cistercian Studies Quarterly, 50*(1), 5–37. Retrieved from http://search.ebscohost.com.naropa.idm.oclc.org/login.aspx?direct=true&db=aph&AN=100879955&site=ehost-live

Utterback, K. T. (2011). Experiencing medieval Christian spirituality. In J. Simmer-Brown and F. Grace (Eds.), *Meditation and the classroom: Contemplative pedagogy for religious studies* (pp. 171–75). Albany: State University of New York Press.

Acknowledgments

This book evidences a synchronicity and a series of events that brought together a group of academics and contemplative practitioners who have used *lectio divina* in both their personal and professional lives, and who have now woven together their differing and complementary interests, energies, and knowledge into a pleasing tapestry. Secular adaptations of *lectio divina* hold promise for broadening educational practice through holistic pedagogy and embodied knowing.

Holistic and embodied pedagogy, in this case, bridges theory and practice, demonstrating the myriad ways that *lectio divina* as a contemplative practice brings into conversation various insights from a range of disciplines, serving to be more inclusive and connect the silos that often separate subject areas and disciplines in K–16 education. *The Whole Person: Embodying Teaching and Learning through* Lectio *and* Visio Divina provides pedagogical examples that deepen and extend learning development of the whole person, integrating body, mind, and spirit to include hearts and minds, making education more inclusive and accessible to all.

We are grateful to all of those with whom we have had the pleasure to work during the development and publication of this book. Without their vision and commitment to contemplative practices and inquiry this book would not be possible. We would like to thank our contributing authors: Elizabeth Hope Dorman, Libby Falk Jones, Daphne Loads, Mary Keator, and Vajra M. Watson. Each author brings a unique practice to illustrate the many ways that this ancient monastic practice can facilitate increased awareness and openness to engaging and educating the whole person in twenty-first-century classrooms, as well as the ways *lectio divina* strengthens personal practices. The students, conference workshop participants, and colleagues who have engaged in *lectio divina* and other contemplative practices with us have made our work possible, and we appreciate their contributions. Last, we would also like to thank our editorial team, Tom Koerner and Emily Tuttle.

We are especially grateful to Michael A. Franklin, chair and professor of the Graduate Art Therapy Program at Naropa University, who wrote the foreword for this book. Through his own lived experience as a visual artist, art therapist, and researcher, he demonstrates how a contemplative practice can facilitate growth and offer embodied wisdom. As the author of *Art as Contemplative Practice* (2018), he explains how both art and contemplative practices cultivate a finely tuned intuitive awareness to "listen, hear, and honor intangible interior processes" (p. xxiv). He understands the power of contemplative practices and contemplative pedagogy for educating the whole person.

We, the editors, are grateful for the collegiality, friendships, and collaborative energies that continue to develop and that have made this book possible. We have deep gratitude for the people, events, and connections that brought us together. Relationships consist of conversations, shared experiences, and mutual interchanges of insights and ideas. Through these collaborative and creative qualities and an ongoing building process, we have presented at national and international conferences, published in peer-reviewed venues together, and ultimately created this book in community with each other. We are honored to curate this collection of chapters, and we look forward to engaging in ongoing conversations with our readers.

Jane E. Dalton
Maureen P. Hall
Catherine E. Hoyser

REFERENCE

Franklin, M. A. (2018). *Art as contemplative practice: Expressive pathways to the self.* Albany, NY: State University of New York Press.

Introduction

In an era of standardized education featuring an overload of information, we as teachers in K–16 need to re-vision how text and images can teach more than skills and content. More specifically, we need also to offer tools for developing personal meaning and significance in the lives of the students we teach. In this book, *lectio divina* is offered as a generative engine for new ideas, personal growth, and development of empathy for the self and for others.

Lewis (2006) warns that there is a danger that our schools will become "soulless" places (p. 69) and argues that a student is viewed as a "brain on a stick" (p. 100). This disturbing image seems to capture what is happening today in K–16 and higher education. As part of the re-visioning of education, *lectio divina* offers pedagogical possibilities for developing the whole person. While current models of standardization promote the separation of minds from bodies, the deep and embodied learning via *lectio divina* weaves them back together and provides new opportunities for humanizing the educational experience.

Further, it is no secret that the humanities are under fire in the twenty-first century (Nussbaum, 2010; Zakaria, 2015). More specifically, Nussbaum underlines, "the humanities and arts provide skills that are essential to keep democracy healthy" (p. xvii). Nussbaum makes clear that the humanities help students to become engaged citizen in a very complex world; a deep understanding of the humanities helps us to imagine life from others' points of view and to think critically. *Lectio divina* offers possibilities for democratizing education through perspective taking and the development of empathy for the human condition.

However, there is hope. As Musil (2015) points out, there is a "countervailing force against such single-minded obsessiveness with jobs as the sole purpose of higher education" (p. 245). Certainly students need to develop themselves for a career, but being educated is much more than just getting a job. Learning, however, should be transformative. By drawing upon the work of others who are investigating the real purpose of higher education, Musil underlines how education involves helping individuals find meaning and purpose in life (Astin, Astin, & Lindholm, 2007) and how becoming civic-minded and caring about the larger community is also central to what it means to be educated.

Practitioner and theorist Jon Kabat-Zinn makes connections between learning, healing, and being ever mindful of the present moment (Kabat-Zinn, 2006); he, too, focuses on the ways in which human beings find themselves in the world, a world best considered as an ongoing and embodied learning environment. Any kind of contemplative practice attempts to integrate all aspects of cognitive and affective learning because that is the way that learners respond and come to understand concepts, ideas, and experiences.

Lectio divina, as an ancient tool for understanding texts, is being excavated from its religious beginnings and re-created in secular forms for twenty-first-century classrooms as a contemplative practice. As Waxler and Hall (2011) point out, "[c]ontemplative practices create an imaginative space in the classroom, a palpable space that allows students to glimpse new possibilities and to experience the connectivity of the human community" (p. 100). Other contemplative practices include active listening, art, yoga, meditation, respectful dialogue, and storytelling, and these, along with *lectio divina*, can be woven into curriculum to foster whole-person learning.

For teachers and students, *lectio divina* offers opportunities for creating transformative learning experiences. These experiences embody content and provide a pedagogical way to weave together and expand students' and teachers' inner lives. *The Whole Person: Embodying Teaching and Learning through* Lectio *and* Visio Divina underlines and demonstrates the importance of educating the entire person. Educating the whole person means nurturing and integrating body, mind, and spirit.

In this book, readers will find a rich collection of voices from diverse settings that illustrate the ways in which *lectio divina* supports growth and learning of the whole person. Each chapter provides in-depth pedagogical strategies modeling how *lectio divina* can be integrated into contemporary classrooms. This integration evidences the transformative impact of *lectio divina*, one that connects students' and teachers' inner lives with the world in which they live. The following paragraphs offer highlights of each of the nine chapters in this book.

In chapter 1, "An Ancient Monastic Practice: Reviving It for a Modern World," Jane E. Dalton, Maureen P. Hall, Catherine E. Hoyser, and Libby Falk Jones provide a history of *lectio divina*, exploring its ancient roots and the ways in which this practice can be reappropriated for transformative teaching and learning in the twenty-first century.

In chapter 2, "Embodying Deep Reading: Mapping Life Experiences through *Lectio Divina*," Maureen P. Hall uses the contemplative pedagogy of *lectio divina* in a graduate education course on critical literacies. Using John Keats's poem "To Autumn" as the text, preservice and in-service teachers experience deep reading and whole person embodied learning through a practice of *lectio divina*.

In chapter 3, "Image and Text: Toward Inner and Outer Wholeness," Jane E. Dalton illustrates the interconnected nature of experience as well as our multidimensionality as human beings. Contemplative practices such as *lectio divina* and *visio divina* invite students and teachers to be present to their own lived experience with greater awareness by allowing meaning to emerge through embodied and creative experiences.

In chapter 4, "*Lectio Divina* and Story-to-Poem Conversion as Tools for Transformative Education," Catherine E. Hoyser shares the benefits of combining the *lectio divina* process with a story-to-poem conversion task. The combination promotes deep reading, deep listening, empathy, and generative literacy and encourages participants to connect with each other. All of these skills build community and enable transformative education.

In chapter 5, "Reading the Word, the Self, the World: *Lectio* and *Visio Divina* as a Gateway to Intellectual and Personal Growth," Libby Falk Jones reveals how practicing *lectio divina* and *visio divina*—dialoguing deeply with a text or image—can lead students to become more aware, to engage challenging ideas, to become more open to possibility, to develop confidence in their own capabilities, and to take joy in learning and creating.

In chapter 6, "Writing about Yoga: *Lectio Divina* and the Awakening of the Soul," Mary Keator describes the way that the contemplative method of *lectio divina* was combined with the literature and practice of yoga to engage students holistically in the subject of yoga and develop their ability to clearly articulate their learning in writing. In the process, students shared their own self-discovery and self-development.

In chapter 7, "*Lectio Divina* as Contemplative, Anti-Oppressive Pedagogy in Social Justice Education Courses," Elizabeth Hope Dorman describes a process that blends contemplative inquiry and reflection within an anti-oppression pedagogy framework that addresses the needs of diverse learners. Through contemplative practice that invites reflection and embodiment, educators are better able to stay in the present moment when faced with discomfort or difficulty and are more likely to become aware of their own multilayered biases and conditioned habits.

In chapter 8, "Embodied Justice: We Are the Divine Text," Vajra M. Watson explores spoken word performance poetry through the lens of divine reading or *lectio divina*. Watson examines classroom practices where life is primary text and students' words are the tableaux of inquiry. She finds that poetic workshops combined with holistic strategies create spaces for personal awakening and collective belonging—the embodiment of a social justice pedagogy.

In chapter 9, "The Restorative Power of *Lectio Divina* and the Arts for University Lecturers," Daphne Loads asserts that in these neoliberal times, academia can feel like a heartless and soulless place. Through practical examples she shows how the transformative power of *lectio divina*, in combination with poetry and artwork, can help lecturers to restore heart and soul to university teaching.

Using *lectio divina* and *visio divina* as pedagogy demands a courageous commitment that strengthens teaching and learning—mind, body, and spirit—through authentic engagement that is compassionate, experiential, and ultimately transformative. The authors in this book demonstrate the value and importance of supporting the inner life in tandem with cognitive and rational ways of being in the world. By adapting this ancient monastic practice into a contemporary pedagogy, these chapters are intended to stimulate a dialogue and offer insights in to the ways transformative pedagogy can engage the whole person.

REFERENCES

Astin, A. W., Astin, H. S., & Lindholm, J. A. (2007). A national study of spirituality in higher education: Students search for meaning and purpose. Higher Education Research Institute, University of California, Los Angeles. Retrieved from http://heri.ucla.edu/index.php.

Kabat-Zinn, J. (2006). *Mindfulness for beginners*. Louisville, CO: Sounds True.

Lewis, H. (2006). *Excellence without a soul? Does liberal education have a future?* New York, NY: Public Affairs.

Musil, C. M. (2015). A step away from complacent knowing: Reinvigorating democracy through the humanities. *Arts and Humanities in Higher Education, 14*, 239–59.

Nussbaum, M. C. (2010). *Not for profit: Why democracy needs the humanities* (Vol. 2). Princeton, NJ: Princeton University Press.

Waxler, R. P., & Hall, M. P. (2011). *Transforming literacy: Changing lives through reading and writing*. Bingley, UK: Emerald.

Zakaria, F. (2015). *In defense of a liberal education*. London: W. W. Norton and Company, Ltd.

Chapter One

An Ancient Monastic Practice

Reviving It for a Modern World

Jane E. Dalton,
University of North Carolina at Charlotte;
Maureen P. Hall,
University of Massachusetts Dartmouth;
Catherine E. Hoyser,
University of Saint Joseph;
Libby Falk Jones,
Berea College

Once a relatively obscure monastic practice, *lectio divina*, a hidden treasure, has emerged with new and exciting contemporary applications as a contemplative practice. Growing from ancient roots, *lectio divina* as a contemplative practice and part of contemplative pedagogy aligns with many efforts in the twenty-first century to investigate how whole persons can be engaged in learning and how they can develop into their best human selves.

In recent years, *lectio divina* and *visio divina* have been modified and made secular for the processes of reading, looking, and contemplating as a way to teach to and from our whole selves. Moreover, *lectio divina* functions as a powerful tool to transform teaching and learning and appreciate its powers to connect fragmented forms of curriculum as a route to the contemplative life, one that recognizes and values all dimensions of being human—mind, body, spirit—which are often overlooked in schools.

Across various disciplines, educators utilize *lectio divina* to read literary texts and *visio divina* for works of art. This type of contemplative education is a humanizing effort designed to create possibilities for students and teachers through which they can find agency and voice and can develop as whole persons. Adopting *lectio divina* in educational settings introduces the approach of savoring and digesting text as a tool to integrate wisdom into our lives through a slow and deliberate method of engaging texts and visual images.

Lectio divina offers a pedagogical process that can manifest deep reading and "can inspire in us a reverence for word and thing and for one another" (Hall, O'Hare, Santavicca, & Jones, 2015, p. 55). *Lectio divina* is embodied learning, a kind that is activated through merging body and mind, a "dynamic process between the outside and the inside, the environment and the self" (Waxler & Hall, 2011, p. 96). Deep reading as an embodied practice "serves to awaken and evoke the reader's voice, helping the learner to make meaning as a whole person immersed in the embodied nature of language" (Hall et al., 2015, p. 49). Through this holistic process of connecting to text, self, and other, *lectio divina* is also a part transformative education. Learning is much more than information; learning is formation and transformation.

Lectio divina as a learning process provides a conduit for creating dialogic spaces for embodied interaction and for transformative experiences where "education can serve as the core of a lifelong journey towards wholeness, rather than merely an accumulation of facts, figures, or skills" (Glazer, 1999, p. 3). More specifically, the fresh ways of understanding *lectio divina* and *visio divina* are needed as a pedagogical teaching of the whole person in an educational system that has become more and more dehumanizing.

In February 2007, more than six hundred participants attended a conference in San Francisco entitled "Uncovering the Heart of Higher Education: Integrative Learning for Compassionate Action in an Interconnected World." Parker Palmer and Arthur Zajonc were two of the main presenters, and their collaboration with Megan Scribner on *The Heart of Higher Education* (2010) grew directly from their embodied conversations at this conference.

In their coauthored book, they reflect on the main questions posed for this conference: "Do current educational efforts address the whole human being—mind, heart, and spirit—in ways that contribute best to our future on this fragile planet? How can we help our colleges and universities become places that awaken the deepest potential in students, faculty, and staff?" (p. 5). Likewise, the work of this book aims to answer these questions by offering *lectio divina* as a transformative approach for educating the whole person.

We offer here a brief historical view of *lectio divina* to understand its origins and its use as a contemplative religious practice before being adapted for secular applications. Furthermore, the history will provide a foundational perspective into the way this approach can be secularized and modified to offer a contemplative and holistic practice in twenty-first-century educational settings.

THE ROOTS OF *LECTIO DIVINA*

The Christian tradition of *lectio divina* originated in the Jewish practice of learning scripture by heart. In Jesus's time, Jews memorized scripture, then repeated the words until they were taken into the heart (Paintner, 2011). Some six hundred years later, St. Benedict, founder of the Benedictine monastery at Monte Cassino and father of Western monasticism, prescribed in his *Rule* daily periods of silent, private, prayerful reading (Casey, 1996). Benedictines regarded sacred reading as essential to spiritual life.

Designed for sacred reading of scripture, *lectio divina* literally refers to "divine reading," which originated as an approach for reading sacred texts. It has sometimes been described as a "methodless method" of prayer, alluding "to the fact that it is less a learned way of prayer than one which spontaneously flows toward contemplation as its destination" (Hall, 1998, p. 9). This practice involves reading or listening that opens gradually to contemplation (Lichtmann, 2005).

Although *lectio divina* means "reading," it is important to note that during the first centuries of the church and after, many Christians could not read (Pennington, 1998). To create a book required hours of very specialized work and resources such as the making of paper and inks as well as the learned skills of writing. Therefore, personal reading was rare because books were scarce and expensive (Casey, 1996). Only texts considered valuable were copied and made available. Thus, texts were approached with confidence in their worth; texts were respected, indeed revered. Furthermore, with the scarcity of texts, oral reading became the means of sharing its words. Therefore, *lectio divina* was more a practice of hearing the word of God (Pennington, 1998, p. 2).

Pennington explains that for the first thousand years of the church, personal reading was primarily hearing the word of God through monks and cleric during the liturgy. The reading was done in a tone that would let the community know the source of text, whether Gospel apostolic writing or patristic commenter, so that the text would become lodged in the memory of the person hearing/listening to the reading. Pennington (1998) explains that at this time,

> text was not divided into words, sentences, and paragraphs, organized to convey concepts immediately through the eye to the brain. This organized way of writing came into practice only after the twelfth century. Rather, there was a row of letters inviting the lips and the tongue to produce particular sounds. It was the *spoken word* that conveyed ideas to the mind. A cloister full of minds during their lectio was aptly spoken of as a community of mumblers. (p. 3)

Much like the reading of poetry today, cadence, rhythm, timing, and complete body engagement would have an effect on the listener. In *lectio divina* it was the recitation of text out loud, speaking with the full presence of the voice (lips and tongue) that moved the listener.

In such reading, the reader's receptivity increases and time slows. Lichtmann describes the process of *lectio divina* as "reverencing the word in all the ways the Word, God's self-expression, manifests itself—in the earth, in human beings, and in being itself" (2005, p. 21). For the early monks, reading was clearly a kind of sacred listening extending to all of creation. St. Benedict explained the *lectio divina* process as "listening with the ear of your heart" (Paintner, 2011, p. 18). This, of course, is not the literal ear but the center of being, the heart, where humans make meaning through a deeper connection with our inner life and the world in which we live (Dalton, 2018).

Lectio divina can be considered straightforward, with its progressive steps experienced as "unified interior movement which reaches the object of its desire fully only in the final contemplation" (Hall, 1998, p.10). Through a four-step process that is slow and reflective, the mind is fully present with the words revealed on the page. *Lectio divina* aids the movement of awareness from the rational and analytical toward a greater wholeness by including the intuitive and emotional ways of knowing (Dalton, 2018).

According to Pennington (1998) one important element of the *lectio divina* practice is a disposition to the practice of faithfulness. He continues, explaining that faithfulness appears in many spiritual traditions:

> Monks and nuns in the Indian tradition wear the kavi, a very simple garment in a bright orange color—what we might call a habit. Its intense color is achieved dipping a piece of white cotton in yellow dye a thousand times. The monastics wear this color as a reminder of their need to dip again and again into the Divine through meditation. (p. 9)

Faithfulness and the practice of full-body engagement with text can also be seen in traditional Jewish or Muslim communities where prayer and gentle movement are entwined (Pennington, 1998). This practice of full immersion and practice with words help to make *lectio divina* remain in the domain of practice. In this sense, *lectio divina*, with the focus on full-body engagement, in secular settings such as higher education moves learning into the domain of experience, practice, and embodied knowing.

THE FOUR MOVEMENTS OF *LECTIO DIVINA*

The four movements of *lectio divina* are not always a sequential or automatic progression. *Lectio divina*, as a secular and contemplative practice, can be adapted and modified in multiple ways across disciplines. Often there is a dance between movements: Silence may precede reading; words before contemplation. The process is about being, letting go, and receiving insights and revelation. *Lectio divina* is an attempt not to fabricate meaning, but to engage and respond to the gift from its first invitation (Hall, p. 32).

The four primary movements of *lectio divina* are: *lectio* (attention), *meditatio* (reflection), *oratio* (receptivity), and *contemplatio* (transformation) (Lichtmann, 2005; Paintner, 2011). What follows is a brief description of the four movements or phases in the *lectio divina* process. The phases may be led by facilitators, or individuals may work through them on their own.

The first phase, *lectio*, simply means "reading." The process for *lectio divina* is to read the text slowly out loud. The listeners are advised to savor the text and to notice the texture of the language, the sounds of the words, and the meaning(s) of the language. Students are requested to listen to the passage for the first time and notice any word or phrase that captures their attention.

In the second or *meditatio* phase, the passage is again read aloud. Participants are asked to see if they can make any personal connections to the text. The facilitators ask participants to allow the text to engage with their inner worlds and personal experiences and to see what meaning may arise. Participants are encouraged to be aware of any thought or reflection that comes to them through this second reading of the passage.

Oratio, the third phase, is where the facilitators ask participants for a response to the passage. Again the passage is read aloud, and again there is a minute of silence after the reading. To help participants identify their responses to the reading, the facilitators may provide a prompt. There may be a particular prompt that is given to participants in order to elicit their response, or the invitation may simply be open to any response. Participants might choose to draw a picture, create a line or two in written response, or act something out.

The fourth phase, *contemplatio*, is about resting in contemplation after the passage has been read aloud for the fourth time. This phase is designed to allow insight or wisdom to come through by just allowing the words to wash over the listeners as they rest in silence. Participants are asked to let go of the words themselves and to consider the broader implications of what can be or has been learned through the passage.

LECTIO DIVINA AND *VISIO DIVINA* AS CONTEMPLATIVE PRACTICE

Lectio divina and *visio divina* offer secular practices based in monastic contemplative practices. Contemplative practices can be broadly defined as "the ways that human beings, across cultures and across time, have found to concentrate, broaden, and deepen conscious awareness as the gateway to cultivating their full potential and to leading more meaningful and fulfilling lives" (Roth, 2006, p. 1788).

Contemplative practices add a missing element in education that serves to enhance the rational and sensory, offering students pragmatic benefits for improving their relationship with themselves, other people, and the world (Dalton, 2016). These practices "have an inward or first-person focus that creates opportunities for greater connection and insight" (Barbezat & Bush, 2014, p. 5) through present-moment awareness; these practices and opportunities are embodied and connect participants with their own interiority. Tobin Hart (2008) underlines the role interiority plays when it comes to education and learning, in that it "involves examining four general dimensions of consciousness related to learning: presence, clarity, detachment, and resilience" (p. 236).

Hart (2008) highlights that "developing interiority may be most valuable not simply as an adjunct to knowledge acquisition but as central and essential to the process of deep and lifelong learning" (p. 247). When interiority is valued in the process of learning and as a way of knowing, teachers can teach to and from the whole person so that individuals are taught with respect to all of their dimensions—mind, body, and spirit.

Moreover, in terms of learning, "contemplative practices are nourished in states of relationality, connectivity, and insight as students learn to build meaningful relationships with self and others" (Keator, 2018, p. 27). Lichtmann (2005) explains that a contemplative approach offers a holistic model for "letting *what is* unfold its level of meaning before us" (p. 13); this approach an important ally in education that further supports the need for educational experiences that embrace and value mind-body-spirit.

Recent empirical studies continue to evidence the power of contemplative education for deepening learning in a range of ways. For example, attentional skills are increased through the contemplative practice of mindfulness (Jennings, 2015; Roeser, Skinner, Beers, & Jennings, 2012; Roeser & Peck, 2009; Schonert-Reichl et al., 2015). Other studies examine potency of deep reading, deep listening, and other activities to support emotional balance, enhance focus, cultivate self-awareness, and promote transformation (Bai, Scott, & Donald, 2009; Hall et al., 2015).

CONTEMPLATIVE PRACTICE AS TRANSFORMATIVE AND HOLISTIC PRACTICE

Teaching and learning are processes of transformation and discovery; *lectio divina* is a conduit for both of these things to happen in education. Drawing on holistic pedagogy as a framework for embodied and transformative experiences, *lectio divina* as a contemplative practice supports an integrated approach to learning and human development. Whether sacred or secular, holistic education offers an educational formula for human beings to grow and develop, to be educated as whole selves.

The foundation of holistic education was formed with philosophers such as Plato and Jean-Jacques Rousseau, who argued that education must address the multiple dimensions of the individual. In the twentieth century, John Dewey and the Progressive movement extended this understanding and viewed education as social integration (Campbell & Simmons, 2012). Holism in contemporary education according to Miller (2000) connects education to personal transformation and self-transcendence, where student development is seen as a merging of social, cultural, and personal experiences that are grounded in real-world concerns.

Miller (2005) explains that "[h]olism is, literally, a search for wholeness in a culture that limits, suppresses, and denies wholeness" (p. 7). The human being is complex and multidimensional, and teaching and learning must not only welcome but invite the many facets of experience into the learning equation. Holistic education differs from other educational approaches because "it focuses on the growth of the whole person, body, mind and soul . . . holistic education, then engages the whole person (Miller, Irwin, & Nigh, 2014, p. 2). Additionally, holistic education draws upon the philosophy that everything in the universe is connected body (Miller, 1993).

Despite being encouraged to become self-directed in our learning as we grow older, societal constraints, culture, and an educational system designed for learning that is based on reward have hampered self-directed growth. This learning through the self resonates with Mezirow's transformative learning theory; he claims, "Our need to understand our experiences is perhaps our most distinctively human attribute. . . . Meaning making is central to what learning is all about" (1991, p. 11). Likewise, *lectio divina* as part of contemplative pedagogy makes space for the meaning-making that Mezirow describes, enabling individuals to speak with their own voice, identifying what is new and dispelling previous assumptions that have been accepted as given.

This transformation through learning "is a movement toward increasing wholeness that simultaneously pushes toward diversity and uniqueness" (Hart, 2000, p. 26). Within the framework of transformative learning theory, education can be understood as the process by which individuals can craft a new or revised interpretation of the meaning of their experience, and by so doing, chart a new course to guide future action. Inviting students and teachers to seek and include deeper, more personal, and perhaps more insightful ways of constructing knowledge offers an alternative route which counters the "banking concept" of teaching and learning that Freire (2004) rails against. *Lectio divina* as a pedagogical method addresses students and teachers as much more than just vessels for receiving information; humans are sentient beings who need an educational process with opportunities for formation and growth.

Palmer, Zajonc, and Scribner (2010) shed light on why holistic education has value from the teacher's perspective; they assert that "by welcoming the whole student into our classes, unfamiliar aspects of who they are and what they care about suddenly come into view" (p. 91). Teaching and learning can offer opportunities for self-directed reflection and growth and learning that Greene (1995) describes as providing an "existential function . . . it provokes a change in the way we view things . . . [and] brings about a transformation in our thinking" (p. 102).

Palmer and other aforementioned educators, theorists, and practitioners argue for a more integrative approach to education, for learning that is grounded within individuals and relationships among individuals (Klein, 2005; Pianta, Hamre, & Allen, 2012). Educational approaches should create openings for teachers and students to explore universal and collective values such as "wisdom, compassion, loving kindness, joy, beauty [and] peacefulness" (Griffin, 1997, p. 271). While other attempts to address improving education focus solely on the curriculum itself, our work weaves together cognitive, social, and emotional dimensions of teaching and learning. Without this, educational process is rendered incomplete and incorrectly designed for the complexity of what it means to be human.

CONCLUSION

We understand *lectio divina* and *visio divina* as a generative engine for new ideas, personal growth, and development of empathy for the self and for others. Throughout this book, authors explore how these ancient practices have newfound relevance for sustaining focus, creating depth and meaning in contemporary classrooms. This book will illustrate the ways in which the ancient practice of *lectio divina* can be applied in a variety of disciplines and content areas. Education is a multidimensional venture, one that draws on the full range of human capacities. Engaging in practices that move us toward our own transformation and realization of the totality of one's lived experience are at the heart of teaching and learning (Dalton 2018).

Furthermore, this work with *lectio divina* is aligned with the tenets of holistic education; it is an evolving tapestry of embodied learning, creating spaces that empower teachers and students to be rooted in their own meaning-making. *Lectio divina* holds power to help people develop agency and voice, all the while deepening their understanding of themselves and others as human beings navigating a hypercomplex world.

ESSENTIAL IDEAS TO CONSIDER

- Contemplative practices enhance rational learning to include embodied sensory experiences.
- *Lectio divina* and *visio divina*, as pedagogical tools for deep reading and seeing, provide opportunities for communal engagement and meaning-making with language.
- As an ancient monastic practice, *lectio divina* has contemporary applications to strengthen learning and humanize education.
- Wholeness in education is defined as mind, body, and spirit and is the foundation of holistic pedagogy.
- Teaching and learning itself is transformation and discovery.

REFERENCES

Bai, H., Scott, C., & Donald, B. (2009). Contemplative pedagogy and revitalization of teacher education. *Alberta Journal of Educational Research, 55*(3).

Barbezat, D. P., & Bush, M. (2014). *Contemplative practices in higher education: Powerful methods to transform teaching and learning.* San Francisco, CA: Jossey-Bass.

Campbell, L., & Simmons, S. (2012). *The heart of art education: Holistic approaches to creativity, integration, and transformation.* Reston, VA: National Art Education Association.

Casey, M. (1996). *Sacred reading: The ancient art of lectio divina.* Liguori, MO: Liguori Publications/HarperCollinsReligious.

Dalton, J. E. (2016). Artfully aware: Contemplative practice in the classroom. *International Journal of Arts & Society: Annual Review, 11.*

Dalton, J. E. (2018). Embracing a contemplative life: Art and teaching as a journey of transformation. In J. E. Dalton, K. Byrnes, & E. Dorman (Eds.), *The teaching self: Contemplative practices and pedagogy in pre-service teacher education* (pp. 13–25). Lanham, MD: Rowman & Littlefield.

Freire, P. (2004). The "banking" concept of education. In A. S. Canestrari & B. A. Marlow (Eds.), *Educational foundations: An anthology of critical readings* (pp. 99–111). London: Sage.

Glazer, S. (Ed.). (1999). *The heart of learning: Spirituality in education.* New York, NY: Tarcher.

Greene, M. (1995). Art and imagination: Reclaiming the sense of possibility. *Phi Delta Kappan, 76*(5), 378–82.

Griffin, D. R. (1997). *Parapsychology, philosophy, and spirituality: A postmodern exploration.* Albany, NY: State University of New York Press.

Hall, M. P., O'Hare, A., Santavicca, N., & Jones, L. F. (2015). The power of deep reading and mindful literacy: An innovative approach in contemporary education. *Innovación Educativa, 15*(67), 49–60.

Hall, T. (1998). *Too deep for words: Rediscovering lectio divina.* Mahwah, NJ: Paulist Press.

Hart, T. (2000). From information to transformation: What the mystics and sages tell us education can be. *Encounter: Education for Meaning and Social Justice, 13*(3), 14–29.

Hart, T. (2008). Interiority and education: Exploring the neurophenomenology of contemplation and its potential role in learning. *Journal of Transformative Education, 6,* 235–50.

Jennings, P. A. (2015). *Mindfulness for teachers: Simple skills for peace and productivity in the classroom* (The Norton Series on the Social Neuroscience of Education). New York, NY: Norton.

Keator, M. (2018). *Lectio divina as contemplative pedagogy: Re-appropriating monastic practice for the humanities*. New York, NY: Routledge.
Klein, J. T. (2005). Integrative learning and interdisciplinary studies. *Peer Review, 7*(4), 8–10.
Lichtmann, M. (2005). *The teacher's way: Teaching and the contemplative life*. New York, NY: Paulist Press.
Mezirow, J. (1991). *Transformative dimensions of adult learning*. San Francisco, CA: Jossey-Bass.
Miller, J. P. (1993). *The holistic teacher*. Toronto, ON: Ontario Institute for Studies in Art Education.
Miller, J. P. (2005). Seeking wholeness. In J. P. Miller, S. Karsten, D. Denton (Eds.), *Holistic learning and spirituality in education: Breaking new ground* (pp. 233–36). Albany, NY: State University of New York Press.
Miller, J. P., Irwin, M., & Nigh, K. (2014). *Teaching from the thinking heart: The practice of holistic education*. Charlotte, NC: Information Age.
Miller, R. (2000). *Caring for new life: Essays on holistic education*. Brandon, VT: Foundation for Educational Renewal.
Paintner, C. V. (2011). *The artist's rule: Nurturing your creative soul with monastic wisdom*. Notre Dame, IN: Sorin Books.
Pennington, M. B. (1998). *Lectio divina: Renewing the ancient practice of praying the scriptures*. New York, NY: Crossroad Publishing.
Palmer, P. J., Zajonc, A., & Scribner, M. (2010). *The heart of higher education: A call to renewal*. San Francisco, CA: Wiley.
Pianta, R. C., Hamre, B. K., & Allen, J. P. (2012). Teacher-student relationships and engagement: Conceptualizing, measuring, and improving the capacity of classroom interactions. In S. L. Christenson, A. L. Reschly, & C. Wylie (Eds.), *Handbook of research on student engagement* (pp. 365–86). New York, NY: Springer.
Roeser, R. W., & Peck, S. C. (2009). An education in awareness: Self, motivation, and self-regulated learning in contemplative perspective. *Educational psychologist, 44*(2), 119–36.
Roeser, R. W., Skinner, E., Beers, J., & Jennings, P. A. (2012). Mindfulness training and teachers' professional development: An emerging area of research and practice. *Child Development Perspectives, 6*(2), 167–73.
Roth, H. (2006). Contemplative studies: Prospects for a new field. *Teachers College Record, 108*(6), 1787–1815.
Schonert-Reichl, K. A., Oberle, E., Lawlor, M. S., Abbott, D., Thomson, K., Oberlander, T., & Diamond, A. (2015). Enhancing cognitive and social-emotional development through a simple-to-administer mindfulness-based school program for elementary school children: A randomized controlled trial. *Developmental Psychology, 51*, 52–66.
Waxler, R. P., & Hall, M. P. (2011). *Transforming literacy: Changing lives through reading and writing*. Bingley, UK: Emerald.

Chapter Two

Embodying Deep Reading

Mapping Life Experiences through Lectio Divina

Maureen P. Hall,
University of Massachusetts Dartmouth

> The soul has been given its own ears, to hear things the mind does not understand. —Rumi

As a society, and in the K–16 schools, there is a resounding call and urgent need for new pedagogical visions and practices, ones that hold promise for humanizing education and moving both teachers and students toward wholeness and their full development as whole persons. Zajonc (2016) argues that "capacities, such as emotional balance and a stable yet flexible attention, are of value both in the classroom and throughout life" (p. 23). Humanizing education can scaffold capacity building, and teachers and learners can underpin creative and innovative thinking, making learners more flexible and adaptable. In order to heed this call for new pedagogical visions, we must bridge theory into practice and create new embodied approaches that work toward humanizing education.

In response to Zajonc's call, this study explores the secular adaptation of the ancient practice of *lectio divina* as a pedagogical intervention to humanize the educational process. More specifically, *lectio divina* was utilized as a contemplative pedagogy in the reading of a poem. The goal was to have students experience embodied reading with *lectio divina* and to gather the results of their experiences by looking at (a) how participants experienced the *lectio divina* classroom activity overall and (b) how participants experienced each step—*lectio, meditatio, oratio,* and *contemplatio*. This study provided an experiment for humanizing the classroom and probed into how this *lectio divina* experience affected participants in terms of the degree to which they were able to feel empathy for and find community with others.

CONTEMPLATIVE PRACTICE AND PEDAGOGY

Contemplative practices and pedagogy involve practices and learning opportunities that occur in the present moment. In terms of learning, "contemplative practices are nourished in states of relationality, connectivity, and insight as students learn to build meaningful relationships with self and others" (Keator, 2018, p. 27). Parker Palmer, a contemplative writer and theorist, underlines contemplative practice as "*any way one has of penetrating illusion and touching reality*" (Palmer, 2015).

In terms of learning, "contemplative practices are nourished in states of relationality, connectivity, and insight as students learn to build meaningful relationships with self and others" (Keator, 2018, p. 27). Contemplative practices and opportunities are embodied and connect participants with others' experiences as well as their own interiority.

One of the problems with education, in times of hyperconnectivity, is that reading, or, more particularly, "deep reading," gets short shrift these days. There is a connection between short attention spans, mind wandering, and the lack of focused attention in educational processes. Students' and teachers' attention spans seem to be shortening and mind wandering is prevalent (Killingsworth & Gilbert, 2010). Though learning may be possible, it is doubtful that deep learning happens in many classroom spaces, as focused attention is needed, and, as Adelman (2014) points out, attention represents a new kind of economy.

In a broader view, integrating contemplative methods in higher education attends to the inner life of students, which is "sorely neglected," as Zajonc (2016) claims. He points out that contemplative methods will "go a long way toward addressing an imbalance increasingly recognized in higher education" (p. 25). In response to Zajonc's call for attention to students' inner lives, this study reports data gathered using *lectio divina* with preservice and in-service teacher education students in a graduate course entitled Critical Literacies. As a contemplative pedagogy, *lectio divina* grows from a secularized version of a sacred and deep reading process.

Although Zajonc pinpoints these needs in higher education, these same needs are palpable in K–12 education. In recent years, *lectio divina* has been utilized and adapted for humanities and social science classrooms (Keator, 2018) with the goal of helping students develop and engage deeply with the text, with the self, and with others. This study documents the adaptation of this literacy technique for preservice and in-service teachers by providing empirical evidence for using *lectio divina* as a communal reading process, one that promotes empathy for self and others, helps to create a community of learners who make embodied meaning of a text and themselves, and provides teachers with new insights about the learning process itself.

DEEP READING: CONNECTIONS TO THE SELF, TO OTHERS, AND TO NEUROSCIENCE

Drawing upon Birkerts's (1994) definition, deep reading is the slowed and thoughtful reading of material with reflection on how the material relates to the self and broader communities. In addition to Birkerts's notions, the field of cognitive neuroscience also contributes to the understanding(s) of deep reading. It has been found, for example, that when an individual engages in deep reading, areas of the brain associated with the conceptualization of the self become more active (e.g., Whitney et al., 2009). In fact, at times the entire brain seems to light up. Such findings support the idea that individuals internalize material that is deeply read and use it as a method for exploring the self and its relation to the larger world.

Additionally, when individuals are relating their personal experiences to the experience of characters in books, the mirror neuron system of the brain becomes active (e.g., Carr, Iacoboni, Dubeau, Mazziotta, & Lenzi, 2003). Theoretically, the act of reading allows readers to deepen their sense of interiority, but through the engagement with language, the reader also gains a deeper understanding of others. Deep reading provides a way to access interiority, as Palmer (2015) suggests, and to activate and promote educational praxis for developing the whole person—body, mind, and spirit.

A JOURNEY OF SECULAR AND CURRICULAR ADAPTATION FOR *LECTIO DIVINA*

Applications of *lectio divina* in secular educational settings still remain limited. However, Keator's recent book *Lectio Divina as Contemplative Pedagogy* (2018) offers great insights into the traditional phases and the possibilities for activating learning in the whole person. This work owes a debt to her, as many ideas in this study draw heavily on her thought-provoking book.

For this intervention, the intended highlight was the "power of education for creating a democratic community," one grounded in the "importance of language and literature, stories and conversation, in the 21st Century classroom" (Waxler & Hall, 2011, p. 1). By utilizing the techniques of *lectio divina*, a contemplative learning experience can be created for the students. In the section below, there are descriptions of each phase of *lectio divina*—

lectio, meditatio, oratio, and *contemplatio*—and what was asked of participants in each.

This study was conducted in a graduate course Critical Literacies (EDU 525), taught at a midsize public university in New England. There were eighteen preservice and in-service teachers as participants. Thirteen of these eighteen were math or science teachers, along with two history teachers, two foreign language teachers, and one English teacher. The course focused on examining language and literacy. Using *lectio divina* in this course represented a way to experience language and make meaning in a social context, and was offered as a model for literacy engagement in a secondary school classroom. The poem chosen for this classroom experience was John Keats's poem "To Autumn" (see appendix A, this volume, pp. 111–12).

Dr. Robert Waxler partnered with me in this *lectio divina* process. He is an English professor and the cofounder of Changing Lives Through Literature (CLTL), which is a literature program and alternative sentencing program for criminal offenders that began in 1991 in southeastern Massachusetts. Waxler's knowledge of Keats's work is considerable, and he was instrumental in leading the participants through a line-by-line understanding of the poem especially in the *lectio* stage but also throughout the whole *lectio divina* process. This was very important because of the different content areas of the participants.

The Four Phases of *Lectio Divina*

The Lectio Phase

Before *lectio divina* is used as an educational process, a poem or short piece of literature needs to be chosen for the experience. Then begins the first phase—*lectio*—which simply refers to "reading." Next, the chosen poem or passage is read aloud by a member of the group. Participants consider the text first in terms of reading/listening: that is, encountering the text, the way it is stitched together.

Readers and listeners are encouraged to notice words and phrases, the rhythm of the language, the punctuation, the way the lines break, and so on—the way the senses are evoked, the beginning of the embodiment of the text through the initial encountering of the text and its ethical demand to pay attention—that is, to read/listen. After the reading of the passage the first time, there is a minute of silence. After this short silent period, participants are asked to identify a word or phrase that sparkled, or captured their attention, and share it with the group.

The Meditatio Phase

Meditatio is the second phase. In this phase the passage is again read aloud. The facilitator invites participants to make connections to the text and asks them to search for meaning. Still, the focus is on the text itself. Participants are tasked to think about what they encounter as the process engages the group to explore further the depth of the text, the emotional and conceptual meaning and implication(s).

Students are asked to analyze, to evoke memory and connection, to see how the words and phrases more deeply fit into clusters, and to feel the way the rhythm calls up further implications. The process here is double: the deepening of the text and the deepening of our understanding of our relationship to the text. This represents a moving to the heart/soul of the text and the heart/soul of ourselves. Again, there is a minute of silence after this second reading of the passage aloud. Participants are asked to find personal connections with the text and to share with the group.

The Oratio Phase

The *oratio* phase involves a response to the passage that has been read. Again the passage is read aloud, and again there is a minute of silence after the reading. To help participants identify their response to the reading, the facilitators may provide a prompt. For our *oratio* phase, participants responded in writing to this prompt: "Write a thank-you note for this poem to John Keats. Pay special attention to something, an idea, a feeling, an emotion.... [W]hat did this poem evoke in you?" Asking participants to write this note of gratitude to Keats was a way to elicit a response and to get them to value what they had reaped from the *oratio* stage.

Just as the *lectio* stage started with attention to the text, participants are now asked to turn their gaze to their subjective response, the response from their own human hearts. This is prayer, or, in a more secular sense, the talking and writing evoked in admiration and the meeting of the heart of the text with our heart expressing thankfulness and gratitude. The inspiration serves as the breath, breathing out in response to having been breathing in.

The Contemplatio Phase

The *contemplatio* phase is the fourth phase. This phase is about resting in contemplation after the passage has been read aloud for the fourth time. This phase is designed to allow insight or wisdom to come through. Participants are invited to let go of the words themselves and to consider the broader implications of what can be or has been learned through the passage.

Many participants now have the experience of wisdom or insight. The experience of wisdom or insight is an internal happening and can include feelings of awe and wonder. These kinds of experiences might be a kind of "surrender," but are, perhaps, the way literature can change life. When the heart of the text and the heart of the reader are joined as one and in community with others—a sense of democracy and universality can be achieved or at least glimpsed. Participants are then asked for a further response. In our *contemplatio* phase, this question was asked: How has all this changed you (the reader), made a difference—through this experience, what has changed? (Keator, 2018). As Lichtmann (2005) points out, *lectio divina* cultivates an "attitude, with which we approach any text or encounter to have it teach us and be changed by it" (p. 34).

A DEEPENING:
STUDENT RESPONSES THROUGH THE *LECTIO DIVINA* PHASES

After the classroom experience, students were given an assignment to write about how they experienced each phase of *lectio divina* as outlined above. Students were instructed to characterize their responses to each phase of the *lectio divina*. This assignment was to write a five-to-seven-page essay about their experiences with *lectio divina* and provide specific examples for how they experienced each phase. The following examples are from student responses to each phase of the *lectio divina* intervention—*lectio*, *meditatio*, *oratio*, and *contemplatio*.

In the *Lectio* Phase

As one can imagine, there was a range of responses to the *lectio* phase of the intervention. In the following section, excerpts from participants' essays about their experiences have been captured. As one participant listened to the poem being read aloud, she noticed how the poem "flowed by its rhyming phrases." In this first *lectio* phase, this student was immediately immersed in the language, started to pay attention to the sounds and the ways in which the language moved, and felt the rhythm of the poem unfolding. There was a stitching together both of elements from the poem and of the participants interacting with one another in community.

Another participant's response also resonated with and showed engagement with the language. This student captured how Keats's poem was engaging and how it "draws us in with its somewhat orderly flow and rhyme . . . with rich words that paint the picture of a beautiful pastoral landscape that we can see, ripe fruit we can taste, the sweetness of honey." This response shows how language created a picture by firing this student's imaginative capacities.

Yet another participant reflected on his experience in being present in the learning process, or how he experienced this embodied learning. He wrote,

"Although I had read the poem the night before, something changed when I heard someone else read it.... I was going on a journey with several people I didn't know very well, and I didn't know the destination." This student noticed a difference, an activation of his imagination, in how he experienced the poem when he read it on his own versus reading it with a group.

One participant experienced the *lectio* phase as a way of paying attention, learning through making meaning in community with others. She wrote, "As we entered the first step, *lectio*, I found that listening to someone else read the poem allowed me to focus more. I was forced to take it at someone else's pace instead of my own. Additionally, hearing the inflection of the reader's voice helped with my understanding and added a bit more meaning to certain parts of the poem that had previously just been words on paper to me."

In the *Meditatio* Phase

In the *meditatio* phase of *lectio divina*, participants were asked to notice what parts of the poem connected to their life experiences and memories and then to share the connection(s) made. More specifically, they were asked to notice any ideas that grew from their experiences with parts of the poem—including images, phrases, or memories that came up. As the *meditatio* practice unfolded, participants began to uncover personal meaning through Keats's use of language. In this *meditatio* phase, deep reading was activated as students began to make deeper meaning by mapping some of their life experiences onto lines and images from poem.

One participant wrote, "In the *meditatio* phase, I was brought back to thinking of my time as a child surrounded by the natural settings of the orchards in Central Massachusetts. As someone who was fortunate to experience the changing seasons that Keats eloquently refers to as a part of my daily life, I can now appreciate the significance this holds in reflecting on the world around us. With the changing seasons as a constant, it is easy to find one's self as part of the same cycle, lingering in the past while drifting onward into the future." Through this phase, this participant relived part of his childhood, found connections, and made meaning.

For another participant, the following lines evoked a memory of her grandfather: "The red-breast whistles from a garden-croft; And gathering swallows twitter in the skies" (lines 10–11). The participant shared a memory of watching her grandfather as "he would sit at his dining room table in the early morning, while watching the birds feed from the birdfeeder in his backyard."

Another student experienced the *meditatio* phase in that it "turned into a moving experience." He described his experience as going "from an intellectual response to a much deeper emotional response," adding that he "got into the deep beauty of the poem. I could see the craft of the poet calling upon universal imagery and language to evoke an emotional and visceral reaction to the formulation of words." In this experience with this poem as art, he shared, "while it did not make me cry, the *lectio divina* did move me at a deep emotional and visceral level."

In the *Oratio* Phase

After the poem was read aloud once more in this stage, participants were given a prompt to write a thank-you note to John Keats, "with special attention to something, an idea, a feeling, an emotion. . . . [W]hat did it evoke in you?"

One participant wrote that the poem reminded her of how her grandfather had immersed her into nature and the natural world. She recalled, "As a young girl, he taught me about nature, as we would go for walks in the woods. . . . [W]e would go blueberry picking or look for a rare flower called 'a lady's slipper.'" She goes on to thank Keats for "time, the time spent over the years with my grandfather I will cherish dearly for the rest of my life." She goes on to show gratitude for her grandfather's teaching, in terms of teaching her that she needs to value time more. She wrote, "I need to take time to slow down and enjoy life as my grandfather did in his 94 years."

Another student's experience with the *oratio* phase was revelatory. As part of the thank-you note to Keats, this participant wrote, "At times, we live in a world where our attention is everywhere and time is limited. . . . He [Keats] reminded me to take things slow, to be 'drows'd with the fume of poppies' and to enjoy what life has to offer—health, love, wisdom, family, friends, opportunities, beauty in nature, etc." For this participant, Keats reminded her to take time, to enjoy life, to slow down.

Yet another participant captured how she experienced the *oratio* phase. She was surprised by her experience, writing, "I was amazed how affected I was by this poem, and thanking him [Keats] was a perfect way to capture this. I used this time to thank Keats for reminding me that we need to slow down in life and enjoy the moment. I, like many people, am in a constant state of busyness and finding time to slow down and focus on what is happening around me is important."

In the *Contemplatio* Phase

In the *contemplatio* phase, participants often experience the insight or wisdom that comes after the *lectio divina* process. In fact, this insight and wisdom might continue to come much later than the reading of the poem and outside of the *lectio divina* classroom session.

Emerging Insight and Wisdom

One participant wrote about the wisdom she gained from the *lectio divina* process and how it had begun to affect her life. She shared that she had "forever developed a feeling of 'awe and wonder'" and that she was changed. She recounted these changes and gave examples, one of which is "taking at least one hour to myself in silence, sometimes looking at the sunset sky . . . to breathe in what I perceive through my senses, to gather my thoughts and then let them go. I have learned to utilize my time more effectively, in a way to have self-care, self-awareness, and self-reflection." She added that she now has moments where she sees herself "not controlling so many of the things around me, but controlling myself, my body, my words, my actions."

Another participant considered this *contemplatio* phase as the phase where there "were the takeaways from the experience." The takeaway for this participant is a new practice; he explained that he is "trying to do deep reading on at least one piece of writing a day." He talked about how he specifically looks for writings that are "not composed lightly. . . and are worth the effort to deep read."

Transcendence

In the *contemplatio* phase, one participant experienced transcendence. He wrote:

> There is that point or that experience that becomes transcendent. In a different way and in a different sense, I experienced that in the *lectio divina*. A concrete example might be helpful. There is one hiking experience that I can still clearly picture. I stopped by the side of a pond and was just taking it all in when a breeze came in over the trees and dropped down to the surface of the pond. It caused ripples in only one small area, only where the wind made contact with the surface of the water. It was like you could see the wind. The *lectio divina* experience took me to that place.

Through engagement with the language and the mapping of memories in nature onto the Keats's poem, this participant found deeper meaning in the poem and mapped it onto life experiences. The *contemplatio* phase is a kind of resting or digesting of meaning-making.

Overall, participants' experiences in the *contemplatio* phase evoked changes in behavior and allowed emotional connections to be made. This phase of *lectio divina* created some inner transformation(s) in many of the participants, allowing them to transcend the teaching and learning space.

Through the *lectio divina* practice, students entered more deeply into the poem. The slow reading allowed time for them to pay attention to its language and rhythm, which awakened their imagination to hearing and seeing the poem in a new light.

As deep readers, they mapped their own life experiences onto the poem, including recalling time spent in nature, cherishing experiences with family members, and slowing down to savor the present moment. By seeing their lives through the lens of the Keats poem and the connections to self and others, like in other phases of *lectio divina*, deep reading was evident and transformational. This firing of the imagination and mapping of life experiences manifested through the embodied experience of *lectio divina* and teaching to the whole person.

CONCLUSION

As Rumi reminds us at the beginning of this chapter, the soul hears things through different ears. *Lectio divina* is a powerful pedagogical approach that opens space to help students "hear through different ears" as it leads students deeper within themselves. Through the deep-reading process of *lectio divina*, participants were transported to places where they were able to connect not only with themselves but with other relationships in their life and with nature, and bring new awareness to these relationships.

One student stated, "It unlocks something." The process allowed them to unlock and open up their varied life experiences, thereby accessing a deeper sense of presence, power, and even wisdom. Likewise, these preservice and in-service teacher participants were moved to unlock their hearing, to hear with new ears and to respond emotionally through the *lectio divina* process with Keats's poem "To Autumn." By accessing their own power as empathic and creative meaning makers, they made emotional connections. They showed empathy for self and others, and shared insights and realizations about their lives having had meaning all along.

Participants used words and phrases like *time*, *looking deeper*, *line by line*, *hidden meaning*, and *interpretation*. It seems like the whole experience of practicing *lectio divina*, which involves slowing down the pace, listening more than once, allowing students to have and own their own experiences with the poem, and empowering students in their own learning process was impactful. The participants gained empowerment through sharing memories and mapping their lives onto the Keats poem and gaining greater awareness of themselves and others through this embodied learning experience.

This *lectio divina* practice with the Keats poem humanized the educational process (teacher and students), by unifying and leading the group toward wholeness and further development as whole human beings. *Lectio divina*, as an embodied learning process, provided participants with new ears, as Rumi reminds us, serving to humanize the teaching and learning space and helping participants to perceive things that minds alone could not hear.

ESSENTIAL IDEAS TO CONSIDER

- As a society and in the K–16 schools, there is an urgent need for new pedagogical visions and practices, ones that hold promise for humanizing education and moving both teachers and students toward wholeness.
- *Lectio divina* provides an embodied pedagogical approach for humanizing education and for moving teachers and students toward their full development as whole persons.
- *Lectio divina* is a communal reading process, one that empowers and promotes empathy for self and others and evokes changes in behavior and perspective.
- Preservice and in-service teachers can gain new insights about the learning process itself through *lectio divina*.

REFERENCES

Adelman, M. (2014). Kindred spirits in teaching contemplative practice: Distraction, solitude, and simplicity. In O. Gunnlaugson, E. W. Sarath, C. Scott, & H. Bai (Eds.), *Contemplative learning and inquiry across disciplines* (pp. 51–68). Albany, NY: State University of New York Press.

Birkerts, S. (1994). *The Gutenberg elegies: The fate of reading in an electronic age.* London, UK: Faber & Faber.

Carr, L., Iacoboni, M., Dubeau, M. C., Mazziotta, J. C., & Lenzi, G. L. (2003). Neural mechanisms of empathy in humans: A relay from neural systems for imitation to limbic areas. *Proceedings of the National Academy of Sciences, 100*(9), 5497–502.

Keator, M. (2018). *Lectio divina as contemplative pedagogy: Re-appropriating monastic practice for the humanities.* New York, NY: Routledge.

Killingsworth, M. A., & Gilbert, D. T. (2010). A wandering mind is an unhappy mind. *Science, 330*(6006), 932–32.

Lichtmann, M. (2005). *The teacher's way: Teaching and the contemplative life.* New York, NY: Paulist.

Palmer, Parker J. (2015, November 11). Contemplative by catastrophe. Retrieved from https://onbeing.org/blog/contemplative-by-catastrophe/

Waxler, R. P. and Hall, M. P. (2011). *Transforming literacy: Changing lives through reading and writing.* Bingley, UK: Emerald.

Whitney, C., Huber, W., Klann, J., Weis, S., Krach, S., & Kircher, T. (2009). Neural correlates of narrative shifts during auditory story comprehension. *Neuroimage, 47*(1), 360–66.

Zajonc, A. (2016). Contemplation in education. In Kimberly A. Schonert-Reichl & Robert W. Roeser (Eds.), *Handbook of mindfulness in education* (pp. 17–28). New York, NY: Springer.

Chapter Three

Image and Text

Toward Inner and Outer Wholeness

Jane E. Dalton,
University of North Carolina at Charlotte

Spiritual teacher Thomas Merton claimed that "there is in all things . . . a hidden wholeness" (Merton & McDonnell, 1974, p. 506). This wholeness can go by many names: "Thomas Merton called it true self. Buddhists call it original nature or big self. Quakers call it the inner teacher or the inner light. Hasidic Jews call it a spark of the divine. Humanists call it identity and integrity. In popular parlance, people often call it soul" (Palmer, 2004, p. 33).

The vision of wholeness connects to an ancient quest with roots in the aforementioned world religions, but also of indigenous cultures, and the American Transcendentalists. Wholeness recognizes the interconnected nature of experience as well as our multidimensionality as human beings.

Palmer (2004) explains that wholeness is always a choice (p. 17). Yet, in modern education students are faced with meeting educational objectives that emphasize cognitive competence and analytical experience at the expense of their emotional and spiritual lives—in short, of their wholeness. This wholeness requires the inner and outer worlds to be in harmony and balanced, integrating all aspects of the individual: mind, body, spirit.

Much of Western education, however, still fails to recognize this wholeness and the ways in which knowledge is constructed. Embodied knowing is an epistemology whereby the body accesses and provides knowledge through a somatic dimension. As Lakoff and Johnson (1999) explain, "Our sense of what is real begins with and depends crucially upon our bodies" (p. 17). Contemplative pedagogy embraces embodied learning, altering the landscape of what constitutes knowledge by adopting first-person introspective methods of inquiry that value inner states of being and knowing (Dalton, 2018a).

Integrating practices into the curriculum that serve to cultivate intuitive and experiential forms of knowing "characterized by wholeness, unity and integration" (Gunnlaugson, 2014, p. 26) expands the capacity for full awareness of the complexities of the human experience. Contemplative practices such as *lectio divina* and *visio divina* invite students and teachers to be present to their own lived experience with greater awareness and provides a deeper connection to the material they study by allowing meaning to emerge through embodied experience.

TRANSFORMING LEARNING THROUGH CONTEMPLATIVE PRACTICES AND VISUAL ART

Contemplative pedagogy and practices evoke a vision of education as transformative, whereby both student and teacher have agency in the learning process. Furthermore, the growth of contemplative pedagogy in higher education is an indicator of the growing emphasis on cultivating the affective in tandem with the cognitive in student growth and learning. These practices can be broadly defined as "the ways that human beings, across cultures and across time, have found to concentrate, broaden, and deepen conscious awareness as the gateway to cultivating their full potential and to leading more meaningful and fulfilling lives" (Roth, 2006, p. 1788).

Contemplative practices offer ways of knowing that weave together the cognitive, the affective, and the spiritual. Learning from and through these perspectives requires shifting educational practices with their current emphasis on *transmission*—wherein a one-way flow of knowledge and skills moves from teacher as authority to student as recipient—to a *transformative* model that recognizes the wholeness of the student (Miller, 2007).

O'Sullivan (2002) explains that transformation means the reorganization of the whole educational system. This reorganization involves "waking up" to or becoming conscious of the interconnections between one's personal, cultural, and environmental identities (Hart, 2001, p.13). One pathway to transforming learning is to offer—and value—embodied knowing that transmutes personal experiences into new meaning. Art, music, and dance provide alternative languages and offer ways of making meaning and drawing attention to the "affective quality and poetry of human experience" (Mezirow, 2000, p. 6).

Dewey (1934) argued in his epic *Art as Experience* that art is a living process that humans experience when a certain quality of attentiveness and emotion is part of the engagement. He argued that the arts develop our ability to perceive and receive the world around us, and in so doing, reframe our personal experience within the larger global context. He explained that experiences are not those singularly viewed from outside, but something that immerses us in our personal stories and social context and contains thoughts, feelings, and sensory awareness.

Combining aesthetic and artistic explorations as a contemplative practice opens students to the complexity of their own experiences and enables them to make connections with the world in which they live, offering deeply personal and rich interpretation for both the maker as well as the viewer. These artistic forms of communication elicit creative responses that transforms learning. As Fowler (1994) explained, "We are creatures of feeling as well as thought, and schools that recognize this basic fact and address it are better schools. Science and technology do not tend to our spirit. The arts do. That is their role" (p. 9).

Including the arts as contemplative practice facilitates transformation, as the arts are deeply embedded with senses and mind/body action and reaction: "a knowing and feeling . . . that includes more of the expansive range of human experience" (Dalton, 2018b, p. 14).

THE ROLE OF EMOTIONAL INTELLIGENCE IN LEARNING

Contemporary education seldom honors the inner lives of individuals as part of everyday reality, yet students bring their whole selves to the classroom. Goleman's (1995) introduction of emotional intelligence moved the inner life and affective domain to the forefront of conversations and has helped educators understand emotional intelligence as a basic requirement for teaching and learning, equal to the development of cognitive skills.

Goleman made the connection between feeling and thinking more explicit by revealing how the brain's emotional and executive areas are interconnected physiologically, especially as they relate to teaching and learning. Lantieri (2008) makes this same connection: "The prefrontal lobes of the brain, which control emotional impulses, are also where working memory resides and where all learning takes place" (p. 17). Deep learning and wholeness can emerge through personal exploration and discovery when cognitive and affective realms are intertwined in the learning environment.

When embodied interactions are privileged in a learning space, whether explained through emotional intelligence or neuroscientific research, there emerges a connectedness that embraces the totality of the human experience, shifting learning away from the siloed approach in which academics and emotional health are segregated. Instead, the emphasis is on the integration of the whole person.

LECTIO DIVINA AND *VISIO DIVINA*: READING AND SEEING THE WORLD

In ancient times, wise men and women fled into the desert to seek solace and solitude to be present with their inner struggles and cultivate inner awareness. Through radical silence, solitude, and continuous prayer, these men and women became known as the desert fathers and mothers who moved through the threshold of their experience a different person (Paintner, 2011, p. x). In higher education, contemplative arts-based practices likewise invite students to move through their personal threshold space to facilitate the transformation of their lives, with the aim of bridging their inner and outer worlds and seeking wholeness.

As a teacher, it is important to be aware of the ways that students can be provided with learning experiences that cultivate time for deeper contemplation through meditation and contemplative based-art experiences. In a world that pushes students toward immediacy and rapidity, giving students permission to move slowly, feel, and attend to both their inner and outer world is not only essential, it is critical. As discussed in the opening chapter to this book, *lectio divina* and *visio divina* represent a secular approach to this Benedictine practice in college classrooms to transform learning and cultivate wholeness.

LECTIO DIVINA: AN ART-BASED PRACTICE

The process of reading slowly, savoring, and allowing words to be "felt" or embodied, is counter to the fast pace of academia. *Lectio divina*, with an added artistic response, provides a slow, mindful approach to embodied knowing. The following section describes an adaptation of the *lectio divina* process, giving voice to meaning-making through visual art. According to Franklin (2017), art as a contemplative practice cultivates a finely tuned intuitive awareness to "listen, hear, and honor intangible interior processes" (p. xxiv). Through making or aesthetic experience, visual art and contemplative practice offers embodied learning that engages physical, sensory, and emotional capacities.

Student Practice: A Visual Response

Using an adaption of *lectio divina* in the classroom that extends the traditional practice of reading scripture as an act of prayer to sentences suitable for meditation or reflection transforms the learning experience into a secular and embodied practice. Zajonc (2008) explains that by ruminating on words they can "lead us beyond the prosaic considerations of conventional life . . . [and] lift us from the usual rounds of thought and speech to deeper reflections" (p.

122). The secularized version of *lectio divina* invites students to read from a variety of texts that can include poetry, inspirational quotes, or short course readings.

In the first step, *lectio*, students may choose to read a sentence out loud if in a private place, or silently in the classroom, without analyzing words but simply hearing or noticing the phrase or words. When reading silently with focused attention, students are invited to be drawn to words that jump off the page, are illuminated, or feel significant in the present moment. They are asked to consider what words pull them and invite deeper reflection. Zajonc (2008) explains that from this point students experience transformation because the words become a part of them, relating to their own lived experience and offering insight that will provide a step forward on the journey of becoming.

In the second step, *meditatio*, students may be asked about how the words and/or phrases relate to their lives and in their growth as students. Students "feel" what they experience and explore understanding and knowing using all human faculties: mind, body, and spirit. This experience of unfolding expands their present-moment awareness, allowing images, symbols, or colors to unfold in their imagination, and sensation in their body, as sources of information.

What follows this is the *oratio* step, where students are invited to respond with visual images using a mixed-media approach in their ongoing class journal sketchbook. They are given free choice to use any techniques or media that represent their visual interpretation of the word or phrase. Student choice of materials may include a variety of wet media such as acrylic paint, watercolors, and gel mediums to lay down a background color or textures, and imagery can be cut from magazines pasted on to the page or drawn by hand.

After reading an article on the benefits of meditation in education, students who soon would be K–12 teachers were asked to create a visual journal response combining imagery and text. Students were asked to reflect on key words or phrases that they felt most inspired them and connected with what they felt was essential for their student experience as they prepared to be K–12 teachers. Two examples are shown in figures 3.1 and 3.2.

Letting the words evoke images allows students to open to intuition and to discovering symbols, shapes, and colors of what was felt and embodied during the reading. Combining an art experience offers a complementary way of knowing, expanding the written word through visual language.

In the final step, *contemplatio*, students reflect and gather insight by writing in their journal connecting the chosen word or text, along with the related art response, to relevant aspects of their life. In this way, this pedagogical innovation allows students to bridge their inner life with the content

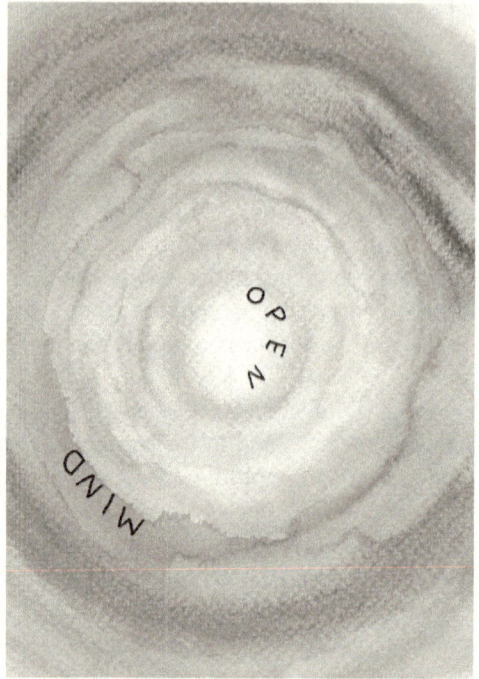

Figure 3.1. Student Work: *Lectio Divina* visual response, 8" x 10"

of their study and to use these words for the cultivation of themselves as whole persons.

Student responses demonstrate a range of experiences that illustrate how learning emerged through a slow, contemplative inquiry. What follows are some example entries from students' journals that speak to cultivating awareness through experience.

> Time is also altered for me when I am in a place of profound engagement with text. I lose track of time and time does not exist in the way it normally does. It is incredibly liberating to not feel bound by the confines of time or living from a scheduled and hectic minute to minute lifestyle as is usual for me during the week.

Allowing students to read text slowly and deliberately cultivated a new understanding and shifting awareness with time.

Another student speaks to a new awareness she has with words. Instead of reading text comprehensively to discern meaning, she experienced how a few words or a phrase can provide insights, connect with a personal experience, and evoke a visual response that deepens learning:

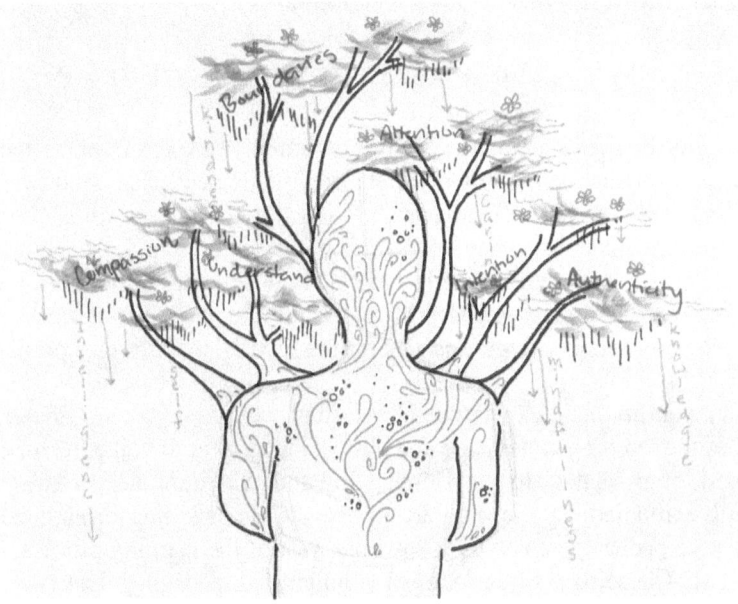

Figure 3.2. Student Work: *Lectio Divina* visual response, 8" x 10"

> *Lectio* [*divina*] also provides an interesting kind of awareness to me. After considering a piece of writing and creating a *lectio* [*divina* visual response] from it, I rarely remember the bulk of the work; *lectio* [*divina*] allows me to zoom in on a tiny passage and pick it apart without being overly influenced by the rest of the work.

Another student, an English major, explains how moving slowly and reading words allowed her to cultivate greater awareness of her emotions:

> *Lectio divina* has also been important in further engaging my love for and sense of connection with words and stories. . . . Becoming more aware of my emotions supports me greatly. It is something I value personally.

But not all students found ease with the *lectio divina* practice. The added step of creating a visual response to the text was challenging, yet in the end it did provide insight for one student into how he interprets words and discerns meaning:

> *Lectio* [*divina*] is a difficult thing for me. While I have a good relationship with words, and typically feel that I can be articulate with my words, I've never had an easy time with drawing. This leads to a lot of difficulty changing words into images, and often my *lectio* [*divina* visual response] projects come

out in a very literal way. In this way, at least the process of *lectio* [*divina*] has informed me of my tendency towards the literal.

VISIO DIVINA: AN AESTHETIC PRACTICE

Just as words offer illumination and transformative experiences, so too can visual images such as paintings, photography, stained glass windows, textiles, and sculpture. All religious traditions value the role of art as a vehicle for experiencing transcendence and illumination through light, color, and images. This is often immediately noticeable when entering into a house of worship, but rich imagery exists in Greek sculpture, Buddhist *thangka* paintings, Navajo sand paintings, and Aboriginal dreamtime paintings, to name a few.

Using an aesthetic experience in a secular way through *visio divina* illuminates the learning experience and allows the student to "take in" an existing work of art as the catalyst for engaging and cultivating deeper awareness through embodied experience. Part of *visio divina* as a transformational and innovative pedagogy involves a slowing down of the learning process. Roberts (2013) describes these learning moments as pedagogy that promotes "deceleration, patience, and immersive attention" (para. 3).

This is a form of "slow looking which means taking the time to carefully observe more than meets the eye at first glance.... [I]t is a form of active cognition with an intrinsically rewarding feedback loop: the more you look, the more you see; the more you see, the more engaged you become" (Tishman, 2017, p. 3).

As a course assignment, students were asked to "behold" one work of art found on campus over a period of five weeks and spend fifteen minutes viewing and being present with the self-selected work of art. The goal was to simply "see." As composer, musician, and philosopher John Cage explains, "Art's purpose is to sober and quiet the mind so that it is in accord with what happens in the world around it, open rather than closed, going in by sitting cross legged, returning to daily experience with a smile" (Brown & Cage, 2000, p. 141). The practice of opening to the art experience in silence enabled students to pay attention to a work of art as a way of being present with the world and with their own lived experience.

This assignment, adapted from a practice offered by art historian Joanna Ziegler (Barbezat & Bush, 2014), used the following steps. Students self-selected a work of art from a list provided of visual art, including sculpture found on campus. During the individual visits, students were to sit in silence in front of the painting or sculpture and simply "behold" what was before them. I encouraged them to go at the same time and same day of the week to create a ritual of repetition of this practice. I also further encouraged them to refrain from reading the wall text or even speaking to others. The instructions were "simply be with the art."

After viewing the art for fifteen minutes, they were then asked to respond in their class journal to several prompts. The first prompts were simply about seeing and not experiencing: What do you see? Describe the shapes, colors, textures, patterns, and so on. Did anything change from visit to visit? It was my hope that by focusing their attention on the visual elements of the work of art, again and again, students would notice changes in the painting as well as within themselves.

After responding to those prompts, students wrote about subjective features of their experience as observers: Write about how you feel physically and emotionally, paying attention to what is going on in your life at this time and how it might impact how you view the work. Where do you notice this experience in your body? Allowing subjectivity in to the learning process was unfamiliar to many students, yet over time they went from not understanding why they were required to look at a work of art repeatedly to actually enjoying this assignment and realizing the benefits.

In their final reflection, students were asked to answer the following question: Did viewing the work continuously shift allegiance from the objective and formal to more subjective experiences and sensations? If so, describe the change—experience, sensations, and relationship to the art, the environment, your perceptions, and so on. As in *lectio divina*, the final phase is to reflect on how this experience and insights connect with the students' life at this moment. The practice of *visio divina* offers the same opportunity for deep reflection that *lectio divina* offers through words. It is the prolonged and repetitive observation that engages cognition and affective modes of learning.

The aim of the "beholding" assignment was to have students notice details and relationships, looking slowly and observing how their own emotional and physical state influenced how work is perceived, and how this perhaps changed with each different visit. Additionally, students came to realize that just because they "looked" at the work of art, they did not necessarily "see it" or understand it: Time and attention were required to wholly comprehend the information the art had to offer. As Tishman (2017) explains, "Intuitive, visual sense-making is necessary in order to move through the world efficiently" (p. 3).

Visio Divina: Students' Experiences

Beholding a work of art provided students with an experience that bridged their inner world of emotions with the outer world of experience, offering another way to move slowly and deliberately and engage deeply with the learning process. Slowing down also proved to offer moments of respite and well-being. Much in the same way that religious art offers transcendent experiences, students' comments such as this one reveal how gazing upon art offered a way of knowing and newfound awareness:

> It seemed tedious at first but eventually it became pretty relaxing to have time to stop thinking about everything going on for fifteen minutes. I did begin to notice my feelings that I was having at the time more because we had to in order to understand why we notice the art different. For instance, I would notice if I was stressed or happy or anxious.

Another student reinforced the sense of emotional awareness that emerged, but also feelings of calm that supported well-being. However, the experience did not solidify until after the final viewing and journal reflection:

> It was interesting how it [perceptions] didn't really alter until afterwards. I didn't notice it at the time but looking back now I am realizing how much mindful awareness was starting to affect me each time I went. I noticed something new and it was really cool to experience. I wasn't really looking forward to going to visit one artwork so many times at first but each time I went I really enjoyed it. It provided me with a break from my hectic life and made me feel calm.

Another student explained how their perception of the artwork changed as well as their understanding of how to view art with more than just a passing glance:

> I definitely noticed a change in my perception of the artwork over time as I started with noticing the big picture, then specific details, then finally put it all together to conclude about what I thought the painting meant. My thoughts about viewing art have changed as I never thought that viewing art multiple times could change the appearance or meaning.

Accessing emotions was difficult for one student. Slow looking, however, did afford a respite in his hectic schedule and provided an experience of embodied knowing he may have not been able to articulate, but that supported his overall learning:

> Observing on a still night, I noticed something new. . . . The especially mirror like pieces stood out more and upon examine I noticed something new. Each color and surface opened a window to a different world. It [beholding] helped me calm me down during stressful times. I would look at the art itself differently.

Well-being may not be a course objective, but the state of students' minds, bodies, and emotions are central to learning. With this assignment, bringing students' wandering attention again back to the object of beholding allowed them to experience a form of self-transformation, whether through emotional awareness, moments of well-being, or deepening ability to focus, feel, and learn through subjective awareness.

Offering students moments of slow pedagogy can reduce the presence of anxiety, boredom, and distraction that greatly reduces students' ability to function effectively and efficiently. Ongoing stress demands a greater need for emotional balance and resilience. Hart (2008) explains, "In a state of chronic stimulation or low-grade anxiety it is difficult to concentrate, step back, and watch ourselves. . . . In other words, our emotional state is significant not only for our well-being but also for our capacity to learn" (p. 14).

CONCLUSION

Contemplative practices such as *lectio divina* and *visio divina* demonstrate a transformative power to strengthen learning. These practices can create an awareness that spills over into students' daily lives, bubbling up at any given moment, expanding their vision and awareness of the present moment. In both practices, students were able to slow down, engage with words and imagery, and cultivate awareness and embodied knowing.

Similarly, these classroom practices appeared to open students up to experiment with and experience wider possibilities for learning through text and visual art. They became more attentive to the experience itself, and this provided a kind of kindling to spark their inner intelligence and raw awareness of the subtle differences found in moment-to-moment experiences. Moreover, students also became aware that knowledge is not always found in books, but also within and through the body.

Addressing the needs of students' emotional, mental, and spiritual lives has become critical in today's statistic-obsessed drive for performance. Our full development as human beings depends upon the ability to express emotions and connect one's emotional and intellectual selves. The contemplative processes of *lectio divina* and *visio divina* have rich potential for merging these important aspects of the self.

ESSENTIAL IDEAS TO CONSIDER

- *Lectio divina* and *visio divina* offer alternative approaches to growth and learning inviting students to be present to their own lived experience with greater awareness.
- The process of reading slowly, savoring, and allowing words to be "felt" or embodied is counter to the fast pace of academia.
- Contemplative practice offers transformational growth that goes beyond cognitive growth to include whole-person knowing.

- Wholeness requires our inner and outer worlds to be in harmony and balance, integrating all aspects of the individual: mind, body, spirit.

REFERENCES

Barbezat, D., & Bush, M. (2014). *Contemplative practices in higher education: Powerful methods to transform teaching and learning.* San Francisco, CA: Jossey-Bass.

Brown, K., and Cage, J. (2000). *John Cage: Visual art: to sober and quiet the mind.* San Francisco, CA: Crown Point Press.

Dalton, J. E. (2018a). Embracing a contemplative life: Art and teaching as a journey of transformation. In J. E. Dalton, K. Byrnes, & E. Dorman (Eds.), *The teaching self: Contemplative practices and pedagogy in pre-service teacher education* (pp. 13–25). Lanham, MD: Rowman & Littlefield.

Dalton, J. E. (2018b). Opening the contemplative mind through art. In Garbutt & N. Roenpagel (Eds.) & A. Rourke and V. Rees (Series Curators), *The mindful eye: Contemplative pedagogies in visual arts education* (pp. 171–85). Transformative pedagogies in the visual domain. Book No. 3. Champaign, IL: Common Ground Research Networks.

Dewey, J. (1934). *Art as experience.* New York, NY: Pedigree.

Fowler, C. (1994). Strong arts, strong schools. *Educational Leadership, 52*(3), 4–9. Retrieved from http://search.proquest.com/docview/62723893/.

Franklin, M. A. (2017). *Art as contemplative practice: Expressive pathways to the SELF.* Albany, NY: State University of New York Press.

Goleman, D. (1995). *Emotional intelligence.* New York, NY: Bantam Books.

Gunnlaugson, O. (2014). *Contemplative learning and inquiry across disciplines.* Albany, NY: State University of New York Press.

Hart, T. (2001). *From information to transformation: Education for the evolution of consciousness.* New York, NY: Peter Lang.

Hart, T. (2008). Interiority and education: Exploring the neurophenomenology of contemplation and its potential role in learning. *Journal of Transformative Education, 6*(4), 235–50.

Lakoff, G., & Johnson, M. (1999). *Philosophy in the flesh: The embodied mind and its challenge to Western thought.* New York, NY: Basic Books.

Lantieri, L, (2008). *Building emotional intelligence: Techniques to cultivate inner strength in children.* Boulder, CO: Sounds True.

Merton, T., & McDonnell, T. C. (1974). *A Thomas Merton reader.* Garden City, NY: Doubleday.

Mezirow, J. (2000). *Learning as transformation: Critical perspectives on a theory in progress* (1st ed.). San Francisco, CA: Jossey-Bass.

Miller, J. P. (2007). *The holistic curriculum.* (2nd ed.). Toronto, ON: University of Toronto Press.

O'Sullivan, E. (2002). The project and vision of transformative education. In E. O'Sullivan, A. Morrell, & M. A. O'Connor (Eds.), *Expanding the boundaries of transformative learning: Essays on theory and praxis* (pp. 1–12). New York, NY: Palgrave.

Paintner, C. V. (2011). *Lectio divina: The sacred art—transforming words and images into heart-centered prayer.* Woodstock, VT: Skylights.

Palmer, P. (2004). *A hidden wholeness: The journey toward an undivided life: Welcoming the soul and weaving community in a wounded world* (1st ed.). San Francisco, CA: Jossey-Bass.

Roberts, J. L. (November/December 2013). The power of patience: Teaching students the value of deceleration and immersive attention. *Harvard.* Retrieved from: http://harvardmagazine.com/profile/Jennifer-L-Roberts.

Roth, H. D. (2006, September 1). Contemplative studies: Prospects for a new field. *Teachers College Record, 108*(9), 1787–815.

Tishman, S. (2017) *Slow looking: The art and practice of learning through observation.* London, UK: Routledge.

Zajonc, A. (2008). *Meditation as contemplative inquiry: When knowing becomes love.* Great Barrington, MA: Lindisfarne Books.

Chapter Four

Lectio Divina and Story-to-Poem Conversion as Tools for Transformative Education

Catherine E. Hoyser,
University of Saint Joseph

In a time when education continues to focus on test results and the world focuses on social media that emphasize differences among people rather than community, society needs pedagogy that educates the whole person by including contemplative and dialogic processes. As Lewis (2006) has so famously written, students have become brains on sticks in the education system. It also would appear that many students have become brains on selfie-sticks because of the preoccupation with their profiles on social media. To counteract these deleterious forces, education needs to implement holistic pedagogy that is transformative. At the heart and center of both transformative learning and *lectio divina* is the intentional work of creating community, trust, and healthy relationships for learning.

One way to increase a sense of community and communication among students and teachers is to pair the deep-reading process of *lectio divina* with the sharing of stories between members of a group. This storytelling entails a face-to-face sharing of personal stories that each listener then converts into a poem or artwork. The process encourages deep listening and dialogue. It challenges assumptions that people may have of each other and the oppression that may result from people jumping to conclusions about the qualities that another individual possesses.

Moreover, following a *lectio divina* process with a story-to-poem exercise combines a deep reading and contemplative activity with a dialogic and deep-listening task that results in both self-reflection and empathy building.

These concepts are rooted in holistic education, where educational development is seen as a merging of social, cultural, and personal experiences that are grounded in real-world concerns (Miller, 2000). To Miller (2005), "[h]olism is, literally, a search for wholeness in a culture that limits, suppresses, and denies wholeness" (p. 7). Empathy is necessary to bridge differences and see commonalities (Greene 2009). We recognize holistic balance of mind, body, and spirit as aspects of the human experience, inviting students and teachers to seek and include deeper, more personal ways of constructing knowledge.

The transformative education leader Jack Mezirow (2003) states that "[c]ommunicative learning refers to understanding what someone means when they communicate with you" (p. 59). The story-to-poem conversion task promotes better communication and metacognition about one's preconceived ideas of oneself as well as of others. Lack of communication can lead to dangerous assumptions and misunderstandings. In fact, the UNESCO holistic education category "Learning to Live Together" recognizes empathy and dialogue that addresses diversity as preventatives to war and conflict (1996). Bridging the differences among students and faculty contributes to building a sense of community commensurate with the UNESCO goals. This transformational work reveals possibilities for educating vital members of a democratic society through the development of imagination, creativity, and expression, helping the participants recognize, as Mezirow calls it, their "problematic frames of reference" (p. 58) and correct misconceptions and assumptions.

In our world today, transformative kinds of learning are needed more than ever; empathetic listening and dialogue can create new understandings of self and other, thereby promoting new ways of seeing the world, recommended by the UNESCO holistic education goals. Moreover, transformative learning opportunities such as *lectio divina* and story-to-poem conversion weave together reflection, which requires trust, with creativity and empathy. Transformative learning activates deepened understanding through dialogic interchange and empathetic listening.

STORY-TO-POEM CONVERSION: A RESEARCH PROJECT

This research, which involves the experiential and contemplative processing of texts and images via *lectio divina* and a dialogic story-to-poem conversion exercise, has been conducted in a variety of educational settings. Those who have experienced this dynamic process include students in higher education settings in the United States and India, K–12 teachers, as well as university professors and administrators. Besides utilizing these exercises in classes, this process has been offered as part of conference presentations. What follows will illustrate this pedagogical innovation of combining *lectio divina* with story-to-poem conversion.

This project transforms the English curriculum and its students from passively learning English for examinations to using language to communicate their life experience with a person that they interact with on a superficial level. Sometimes students do not interact at all with each other except for sitting in class together. Usually they do not talk to each other and are looking at their phones instead. The result of these combined tasks of deep reading, deep listening, and poem writing tasks is a deepening of relationships, a building of a classroom community, and an increasing empathy for others.

One example may suffice to show how this experiential process promotes empathy and transformation. A teacher from a rural southern school system in the United States was paired with a graduate student who was brought over from China when he was five years old. The schoolteacher taught in a system that did not have international students. As partners, each wrote a poem about the story the other shared. The teacher captured the emotion of the student's arrival in the United States having not seen his mother for three years. Through this interchange, and in the poems, they demonstrated that each was moved by the other's story. By listening to each other's story, their assumptions about one another were changed. This process evoked empathy and created community between them. At the center of transformative education lies the expansion of community, which is essential to the learning experience. This approach aligns with transformative learning; as Mezirow (2003) wrote, "Transformative learning is learning that transforms problematic frames of reference—sets of fixed assumptions and expectations . . . to make them more inclusive, discriminating, open, reflective, and emotionally able to change" (p. 58). The deep reading of *lectio divina* transforms the individual's relation to the self; the deep listening and generative literacy, the using of words significant to the storyteller or poem writer, and the storytelling-to-poem conversion transform the relation of the self with others.

TELLING STORIES: BUILDING COMMUNITY

Contemplative education fosters the development of the whole person. Furthermore, the story-to-poem process following the *lectio divina* connects the interior and emotional perceptions from the *lectio divina* to the interpersonal relationship of deep listening and sharing. As Keator (2018) argues, "When human beings learn to listen to their inner self in conversation with others, they can begin to discover hidden possibilities for the transformation of humanity and the world we inhabit together" (p. 5). She elaborates that "contemplative practices are nourished in states of relationship, connectivity, and insight as students learn to build meaningful relationships with self and others" (p. 27). This process of developing relationship with self and others can contribute to the UNESCO goals for world peace and conflict avoidance.

Slowing down the reading process via *lectio divina* and increasing listening skills as well as empathy via the story-to-poem conversion exercise engages the whole person and transforms the educational process into the personal and communal. Others, including Palmer (1998), underline the importance of community as it enables both teachers and students to feel safe in the classroom and more able to focus on the learning itself. The creation of community is intentional work, a conscious effort for a safe space and communication. When the learning environment has been intentionally created so that the quality of interactions is healthy and interdependent, deeper learning can manifest.

In fact, Rodriguez (2018) has found that students telling their story has shown more "common experiences and community building rather than chronicling differences" in his Educational Journey project with minoritized youth (p. 5). Additionally, the storytelling has helped break the oppression of colonialism, slavery, and injustice (ibid.). The insights from *lectio divina* paired with the story-to-poem conversion process enhance the opportunities for challenging oppression and building community while fostering empathy and peaceful communication.

The sharing of stories about one's experiences in dialogue with others is already being used for reconciliation in Northern Ireland, where individuals from opposite sides of the issue during "The Troubles" tell stories about themselves to each other. A similar program exists between Israelis and Palestinians. Our process adds *lectio divina* and the generative literacy activity of creating a poem about the story each person has heard during a dialogic exchange. We believe these additions encourage deeper reflection, listening, and empathy.

Integrating the creative processes of Hamma's (2002) four-step *lectio divina* and story-to-poem conversion as methods for K–16 students into the curriculum helps students communicate across identities to develop a sense of community and increase empathy toward others. The deep reading involved in this and the other steps helps individuals to find meaning, know themselves, and connect to others (Barbezat & Bush, 2013). As Birkerts (1994) has defined it, "Reading, because we control it, is adaptable to our needs and rhythms. We are free to indulge our subjective associative impulse; the term I coin for this is deep reading" (p. 38). In fact, the deep-reading process of *lectio divina* has the potential to develop attentional skills, to be thoughtful and fully aware of others while embracing one's own identity (Hall, O'Hare, Santavicca, & Jones, 2015). Wolf's recent book *Reader Come Home* (2018) connects deep reading as a crucial means of maintaining democracy in the face of social media.

Members of one workshop came from a variety of fields; among them were university faculty and graduate students. Attendees participated in two exercises: contemplative processing and deep reading of texts via *lectio divina*, followed by generative literacy and community building via the story-to-poem conversion exercise of deep listening based on the *lectio divina* practice. Participants returned to their classrooms with an expanded repertoire of methods to foster community and communication that transforms their students' education and lives.

LECTIO DIVINA STORY-TO-POEM CONVERSION: THE PROCESS

In one conference experiential session, participants read out loud Ladinsky's translation of the poet Hafiz's (2002) poem "At This Party" for each step of the *lectio divina* portion of the exercise, based on Hamma's (2002) secularized *lectio divina* steps of paying attention (*lectio*), pondering (*meditatio*), responding (*oratio*), and surrendering (*contemplatio*). After each of the four readings, individuals shared the words or phrases that resonated with them. Upon completion of this process, participants paired up and shared stories about their experience during the *lectio divina*. As one person spoke, the other had to listen deeply without interruption or questions to grasp the significance of the speaker's experience. Listeners were not allowed to take notes, but instead had to concentrate closely on what they were hearing. After the sharing of stories, each participant wrote a poem or drew a response to the story his or her partner shared.

Lectio

The first step of the process was one person reading "At This Party" out loud to the entire group. Participants were told not to take notes, just to listen and pay attention to words or phrases that resonated with them on an emotional rather than intellectual level. They could also see the poem on the PowerPoint slide at the front of the room. A minute's pause for reflection followed the reading. Participants shared orally with the entire group a variety of words or images that resonated with them on some level. *The soul, bowls*, and *Hell* were words that evoked the most response, primarily because of their spiritual connotations. Inviting more people to the party captured some respondents' attention also.

Meditatio

In the second step, participants reflected on other words that caught their attention during the second oral reading of the poem, pondered new insights, and connected their responses to their own experiences. Again, *soul, Hell,* and *bowls* piqued the listeners' interest. In addition, however, the words *secrets* and *sharing* entered into the pool of words that called to them. They spoke about the significance of those images and words for themselves personally and in the poem. One participant shared that *soul* and *Hell* evoked her religious upbringing and thoughts about spiritual damnation rather than a party.

Oratio

After the third reading of the poem, participants wrote their reactions to the phrases or words that moved them. They were given ten minutes to do so. Participants responded orally by sharing their written responses to the language that caught them during this reading. Their sharing ranged from noticing a strong reaction to the word *Hell* in the middle of a poem about a party to enjoying the expansiveness of inviting more people.

Contemplatio

The final reading of the poem presented the group the opportunity to rest in the words and the feelings that the poem evoked. Again, they were asked to connect their reactions to "At This Party" by identifying scenes, memories, or circumstances from their life that the poem's language elicited. Instead of debriefing as a whole group, participants paired up and shared stories based on their reflections, which is the first step of the second exercise.

Story-to-Poem Conversion

After completing the *lectio divina* process of deep reading and reflection, participants proceeded to share their stories in pairs and create reactions to the stories they heard. These next steps develop empathy and generative literacy that are essential for community building, as Greene (2000), Waxler (2014), and Freire and Macedo (2005) argue. The psychologist Jerome Bruner (1991) posited that we understand our lives as story. McAdams (1993) developed Bruner's theories about humans defining themselves through narrative further, claiming that "[w]e are born with a narrating mind" (p. 28). In fact, as Waxler (2014) reminds us, we are all striving "to create a life story. . . . We need story to contextualize our contingent experiences, and we need that imagined context to create and interpret the ongoing story of our 'real lives'" (pp. 8–9). In our media-dominated society, listening carefully and thoughtfully has slipped away to be replaced by sound bites and tweets.

The deep reading of Hafiz's poem shifts to a deep-listening process that then leads to the creation of a poem. Extending the reading to a storytelling exercise demands that one student must listen to the other's story, process the significance of that story for the speaker, and create an imaginative rendering in poetry of the other person's emotional experience. These combined experiences result in the creation of a community rather than a collection of segregated individuals just sitting in the classroom. The "dialogic stance" in the literacy classroom recognizes that students arrive with prior experience and knowledge that they can share with others (Fecho, 2011, pp. 23–24). This approach toward the students promotes a sense of respect for each person's narrative and empowers participants to acknowledge the stories they have constructed of their lives.

This work draws on Freire and Macedo's (2005) notions of literacy and power in that learning to listen to someone else's story and to engage in respectful dialogue promotes the development of empathy and empowers people to communicate thoughtfully and create coalition rather than division. In fact, the process of telling a story and listening to a story is a collaborative effort on the part of both participants. The cognitive researcher Mark Turner describes the process as: "It's not just speakers who make up a story as it goes along, but listeners to some extent do, too, by determining the gist, the central patterns, then filling in the meaning of the words that streaked by. Storytelling is a collaboration between listener and teller" (Rich, 2010, p. 134). With this collaboration, community is built.

Step 1: Storytelling

We asked participants to pair up and proceed to tell each other a story based on their individual reactions to Hafiz's poem and the *lectio divina* deep reading. Members of the pairs had five minutes each to share their narratives. (The timing of each step of the exercise depends on the amount of time available.) Each person had to listen to the other's story without taking notes. Letting go of the crutch of note-taking is more difficult than we think it is. Many people struggle with anxiety about not getting something "right" if they do not take notes. This step forces participants to listen for the emotional resonance of the events in the story rather than absolute accuracy of the details.

Not taking notes forces listeners into a deep-listening mode that they would not otherwise engage in because of the distraction of taking correct notes. Moreover, because participants know that they must create poems based on what they are hearing, they have the motivation to listen carefully. If listening to the story were the last step, they would lose the extra focus that they need to understand and empathize with the storyteller's narrative in order to create a poem.

Step 2: Writing the Poem

After the partners completed their story sharing, they wrote responses to what they heard. We instructed them to allow themselves to mind map, draw, or list ideas and words before they began creating their poem. Additionally, they could choose to include both their story and their partners in a poem to mix the two together or write only about their partner's. They were not to write about their own story only. One individual created a chart or mind map of words and emotions the storyteller expressed before she wrote her poem. Participants were encouraged to write a list poem, free verse, haiku, or any form they felt motivated to use for their poem. Instructors might share samples of these forms before beginning the *lectio divina* and story-to-poem conversion process.

Step 3: Sharing

Participants voluntarily shared the draft poems they had composed as a result of their deep listening to their partner's story response to the *lectio divina* process. One author's poem exemplifies the focus on the bowls:

> Empty bowls—
> Many empty bowls—
> The party-giver is not filling them,
> Asking, rather, that the guests bring wine
> To the party.
> Why?
> And why are there many bowls
> Rather than one great bowl
> Into which we pour the wine we bring?
> —Kathleen Goodyear

This poem reflects the storyteller's pondering about the role of the guests, the multiple bowls as opposed to one central communal bowl, and the emptiness of the bowls; our discussion had focused on this choice by Hafiz.

Another participant created haiku in response to the story she heard. The thread of community and communion dominates her poems. Her first haiku emphasizes isolation that becomes resolved:

> This is your table
> I am not yet welcome there
> Please join me at mine.

For the second haiku, communion with frustration echoes Hafiz's poem's narrative:

> Encountering you
> Longing for communion with
> We cannot meet here.
> —Shakiyla Smith

These haiku reveal the listener/author responding with empathy to the story to which she listened deeply. She recognizes the storyteller's sense of isolation that moves into an invitation to join community.

The creator of the mind map wrote a poem that begins with the word *community* and repeats it multiple times, including in three anaphoric lines that begin with the word. She lists the different types of community the storyteller apparently described in her story. At the end, the poet asks, "I wonder what is hiding behind the need/to build a community/And I wonder what is behind this curtain."

In the discussion after the poem sharing, one person observed that community was a thread throughout all of the writing, despite the differences in the poetry and among the people in the group. Hafiz's poem, however, does not include that word and is, in fact, a complaint to his listener about his or her lack of sharing secrets and helping to entertain people.

The speaker in the poem argues that he has to do all of the work when there is a party and tell the stories, but if the listener shared secrets as well, they could invite more people. The bowls would be filled. Another person in the first poem example wondered about Hafiz's use of individual bowls rather than one communal bowl at the party. As mentioned earlier, developing relationship with self and others through this process holds promise as a way to promote world peace and conflict avoidance. One can conclude that the individual reflections coupled with the sharing of the contemplative experience of *lectio divina* connected participants to each other as a community and, by extension, to the greater world or global community.

CONCLUSION

In many ways, community is the linchpin allowing for healthy interdependent relationships along with the focused attention students need when they accomplish the hard work of reflection and other learning tasks. Likewise, community is essential to creating transformative learning experiences. The respectful dialogue and deep listening that are required in the *lectio divina* and story-to-poem interchanges deepen empathy, moving participants into a sense of community. The generative literacy that creates the reflections, art, and poetry feeds empathy and epitomizes transformative education.

Lectio divina and story-to-poem activates creativity, imagination, and reflection, which are all essential to healing a conflicted world. These learning experiences also activate the imagination through the process of creating poems, stories, and drawings. This is the kind of transformative learning we need; we see this as a kind of generative literacy. As Dalton (2018) argues, "*Lectio divina* aids the movement of awareness from the rational and analytical toward a greater wholeness by including the intuitive and emotional ways of knowing" (p. 18). Building community via transformative learning processes and making a positive difference are crucial in a particularly contentious world. Recognizing that students and faculty do not leave their emotions and life stories at the door of the classroom, but instead bring all of themselves into the room, is crucial to healthy interactions and positive learning in a trusting community.

This research knits together Mezirow's (2003) notions of changing one's frame of reference via story-to-poem conversion and looking at something differently via *lectio divina*. Even though Mezirow's original work was geared specifically toward adult learners, we see that transformative learning holds possibilities for a range of learners. Through transformative learning as a conduit, students and teachers can continue to find ways to understand previous experiences in new lights and to view these experiences through different frames of reference.

Lectio divina and story-to-poem conversion provide insights that can help us all learn to live together in community and actually to transform through learning experiences. The author bell hooks (1994) shares that Thich Nhat Hanh's focus on holistic education, which meant a unity of mind, body, and spirit, taught her a revolutionary approach to pedagogy and to recognizing the role of the teacher as healer. Our combination of deep reading and inner reflection via *lectio divina* and deep listening, responsive writing, and empathy in response to another person provides another set of opportunities for healing our students and community.

ESSENTIAL IDEAS TO CONSIDER

- *Lectio divina* empowers students' ability to focus, concentrate, and reflect on their reading.
- Deep listening results in both self-reflection and empathy building.
- *Lectio divina* combined with story-to-poem conversion merges two powerful methods of engaging students in developing self-reflection, deep-reading skills, generative literacy, and empathy.

- Developing habits of self-reflection, empathy, and communication within the classroom builds community and promotes the development of the whole person.
- The generative literacy of story-to-poem conversion provides an embodied learning experience that fosters communication and empathy.

REFERENCES

Barbezat, D. P., & Bush, M. (2013). *Contemplative practices in higher education: Powerful methods to transform teaching and learning.* Hoboken, NJ: Wiley.

Birkerts, S. (1994). *The Gutenberg elegies: The fate of reading in an electronic age.* London: Faber & Faber.

Bruner, J. (1991). The narrative construction of reality. *Critical Inquiry, 18*(1), 1–21.

Dalton, J. (2018). Embracing a contemplative life: Art and teaching as a journey of transformation. In J. E. Dalton, E. H. Dorman, & K. Byrnes (Eds.), *The teaching self: Contemplative practices, pedagogy, and research in education* (pp. 13–25). Lanham, MD: Rowman & Littlefield.

Fecho, B. (2011). *Teaching for the students: Habits of heart, mind, and practice in the engaged classroom.* New York, NY: Teachers College Press.

Freire, P., & Macedo, D. (2005). *Literacy: Reading the word and the world.* London: Routledge.

Greene, M. (2000). *Releasing the imagination: Essays on education, the arts, and social change.* San Francisco, CA: Jossey-Bass.

Greene, M. (2009). In search of a critical pedagogy. In A. Darder, M. Baltodano, & R. D. Torres (Eds.), *The critical pedagogy reader* (pp. 97–112). New York, NY: Routledge. (Originally published 1986 in *Harvard Educational Review, 56*(4), 427–41.)

Hafiz (2002). At this party. In D. Ladinsky (Trans.), *The subject tonight is love: 60 wild and sweet poems* (p. 6). New York, NY: Penguin Putnam.

Hall, M. P., O'Hare, A., Santavicca, N., & Jones, L. F. (2015). The power of deep reading and mindful literacy: An innovative approach in contemporary education. *Innovacion Educativa, 15*(67), 49–60.

Hamma, R. M. (2002). *Earth's echo: Sacred encounters with nature.* Notre Dame, IN: Sorin Books.

hooks, b. (1994). *Teaching to transgress: Education as the practice of freedom.* New York, NY: Routledge.

Keator, M. (2018). *Lectio divina as contemplative prdagogy: Re-appropriating monastic practice for the humanities.* Routledge Research in Education Book 16. New York, NY: Routledge.

Lewis, H. (2006). *Excellence without a soul? Does liberal education have a future?* New York, NY: Public Affairs.

McAdams, D. P. (1993). *The stories we live by: Personal myths and the making of the self.* New York, NY: Guilford Press.

Mezirow, J. (2003). Transformative learning as discourse. *Journal of Transformative Education, 1*(1), 58–63.

Miller, J. P. (2005). Introduction: Holistic learning. In Miller, J. P., Karsten, S., Denton, D., Orr, D., & Coladillo Kates, I. (Eds.), *Holistic learning and spirituality in education: Breaking new ground.* Albany, NY: State University of New York Press.

Miller, R. (2000). *Caring for a new life: Essays on holistic education.* Brandon, VT: Foundation for Educational Renewal.

Palmer, P. J. (1998). *The courage to teach: A guide for reflection and renewal.* San Francisco, CA: Jossey-Bass.

Rich, K. R. (2010). *Dreaming in Hindi: Coming awake in another language.* New York, NY: Houghton Mifflin Harcourt.

Rodriguez, L. F. (2018). The educational journeys of students of color across the educational pipeline: A pedagogy of storytelling or a struggle for freedom? *Diaspora, indigenous, and minority education, 12*(4), 214–29. Retrieved from https://doi.org/10.1080/15595692.2018.1497970.

UNESCO. (1996). The four pillars of education. In *Learning: The treasure within: Report to UNESCO of the international commission on education for the twenty-first century*. Paris: UNESCO.

Waxler, R. P. (2014). *The risks of reading: How literature helps us understand ourselves and the world*. New York, NY: Bloomsbury.

Wolf, M. (2018). *Reader come home: The reading brain in a digital world*. New York, NY: Harper.

Chapter Five

Reading the Word, the Self, the World

Lectio *and* Visio Divina *as a Gateway to Intellectual and Personal Growth*

Libby Falk Jones,
Berea College

> Reading Rilke's *Letters to a Young Poet* is like a lifeboat for the good and the beautiful in yourself. Being a sensitive watcher and a contemplative thinker in these harsh times is really ugly and difficult and that book was really helpful in that. —Contemplative writing student

Lectio divina, as Chittister (2011) describes it, can be an uncomfortable process. The reading of a small passage or the viewing of an image (*visio divina*) initiates a soul wrestling, a challenging, often wrenching dive within, opening to what may be painful self-knowledge. Yet this process of slow, contemplative scrutiny can lead, finally, to the deep knowledge necessary for the intellectual, emotional, and spiritual growth that constitutes wholeness (pp. 76–77).

Contemplative approaches, including meditative reading and seeing, are central to an advanced, self-selected writing class that has enrolled nearly one hundred Berea College students since 2009. Berea, a comprehensive liberal arts college in the foothills of Appalachia, serves students of great promise whose limited financial resources typically preclude getting a quality liberal arts education. In return for their full-tuition scholarships, students are required to work at least twelve hours a week for the college.

With classes, labor, activities, and other personal responsibilities, Berea students experience weekly workloads that leave little time for periods of silence, solitude, and deep reflection. Yet such an environment is precisely what writers need to deepen in order to develop their vision and extend their craft. The goal of contemplative writing has been to create a place of retreat where writers can work alone and together to explore inner and outer worlds.

Practices of meditative reading and seeing have become central elements in this course. These practices have helped students develop focus, take on challenging questions, make discoveries, and uncover elements of themselves they thought had been lost. Engaging in contemplative reading and seeing practices has also led students to explore various writing techniques and extend their knowledge of craft. In-depth interviews with more than thirty students from different contemplative writing classes, conducted one to six years following the course's conclusion, suggest that contemplative approaches, including contemplative reading and seeing, have led to substantial intellectual and personal development and to lasting holistic learning.

MINDFUL READING AND SEEING: CONCEPTS AND PROCESSES

Contemplative reading and seeing can be understood as paying close attention to a text or image, a form of listening where the reader heightens her awareness on multiple levels (Lichtmann, 2005; Miller & Hughes, 2012). The reader/viewer engages in a four-part process:

- reading/seeing (engaging the passage or image);
- pondering (letting the passage or image speak in a variety of ways, meditating on it with one's "reason, imagination, and will" (Anthony, 1995, p. 9);
- responding (offering something of oneself, in a variety of forms); and
- contemplating (pulling threads together or creating a prayer or mantra to take away; Hall, O'Hare, Santavicca, & Jones, 2015; Hamma, 2002; Lichtmann, 2005).

This process of working with a passage or an image thus honors a creator's words or picture while also encouraging and valuing one's own experiences and insights. The text or image becomes not static but deeply dialogic, imbued with "a fluid and responsive quality" (Paintner, 2012, p. 5). Implicit in contemplative reading and seeing is the concept of rereading and re-viewing, of encountering text or image over time and from many viewpoints. What takes the reader's or seer's initial attention becomes the beginning of a relationship. A second, third, or fifth reading yields new and deeper insights into the text or image as well as into the self who is reading or viewing.

CHOOSING TEXTS AND IMAGES FOR *LECTIO*

To practice *lectio*, no text or image need be excluded—the way of reading or seeing is what matters. Though *lectio divina* began as a Benedictine practice where monks read or heard scripture, even then texts other than scripture were offered. These included founders' sayings, scriptural commentaries, and words by other respected writers. Subjects for *visio divina* in medieval times included not only stained glass windows depicting scripture, but architecture and statuary—various elements of creation, all of which were considered sacred experiences (Hamma, 2002).

When spiritual texts are chosen, they may come from any spiritual or wisdom tradition. "Reading" may take the form of movement: Several contemplative writing students experienced the meditative walking of a labyrinth as a kind of reading. Another appropriate text is a piece of one's own writing, reviewed over time. Many students practiced contemplative seeing through making and journaling about photographs, guided by Zehr's (2005) *Little Book of Contemplative Photography*. Whatever the text or image, it is the process of reading or seeing that becomes significant, through the deep attention and awareness the reader brings to the work.

Key to engaging in *lectio divina* and *visio divina* is understanding that less can be more. Rather than attempting to ingest quantities of words and ideas, the reader works with a small piece of text or a single image. One student described his reading as "chipping away" at a book. Another wrote extensively about the ambiguity she discovered as she studied a photograph she had made (Jones, 2018).

ENCOUNTERING TEXTS AND IMAGES

How the text or image is encountered is central to *lectio* or *visio divina*. Taking time to center (O'Reilley, in Miller & Hughes, 2012) and claiming silence help the reader to focus. Reading slowly and pausing is also important. One contemplative writing student described her process: "I just look up and I read a line or a page and just sit like that."

The goal of *lectio* or *visio divina* is engaging the text or image without initially imposing one's own self or frame upon it. Sher (2002) describes this as being a "yin" listener, one who is empty, ready to be filled by another's words (p. 127). One contemplative writing student described her process in these terms: "It was just me calling out and me being open and receptive and receiving."

This engagement is a kind of physical entering-in, or as described by William of St. Thierry (1971), a twelfth-century Cistercian abbot, as "taken . . . into the stomach, to be more carefully digested" (pp. 51–52). Reading a text aloud is one means of making words more tangible and present. Memorizing a poem or passage is a particularly effective means of taking in a text. Brother Paul Quenon (2018), who has spent more than fifty years as a monk at the Abbey of Gethsemani in Kentucky, carries this metaphor forward when he speaks of the power of memorizing poetry: "It is not enough to get poetry inside your skull. It has physicality and sound that require putting it under your belt, ingesting and getting it inside your body" (p. 56).

Today, images may be created and "memorized" through repeated study, often via the use of a cell phone camera. Keeping open to the possibilities the text or image suggests is also important. Unlike "reading to find a particular idea or support a thesis, the reader engaged in *lectio divina* stays aware and patient, noticing without pre-judging" (O'Reilley, qtd. in Miller & Hughes, 2012). A student described *lectio divina* as an experience of openness, of permission: "You are just reading for the act and for the mulling over and not being so analytical. . . . I never felt like I had to force out anything." Students practicing *visio divina* through photography spoke of images calling to them to be made (Jones, 2018). Reading and seeing thus become processes of discovery (ibid.).

Rereading a text or looking repeatedly at an image becomes a powerful means of developing depth in understanding and in responding. Rereading during the term, or even afterward, can yield extra insights. One student, taking the contemplative writing course as an independent study while abroad in Japan, read a writing text he had chosen two more times in the four years following the course. His rereadings allowed him to reconnect with experiences in Japan and then, as he entered work as an educational professional, to reconnect with his creative self. For this student, the one text became a symphony as it spoke to him in different ways.

CONTEMPLATIVE READING AND SEEING: OUTCOMES

Engaging in *lectio* or *visio divina* contributed to students' intellectual and personal growth in a variety of ways. Countering the isolationist tendencies in education today, reading and seeing worked to help students develop a web of connections to the writers they read, to nature, to their deeper or earlier selves, and to one another. These practices also helped students push past boundaries to become more creative and rekindled their joy in engaging with texts and images and in making art.

Making and Deepening Connections

Every class has engaged some writings by Thomas Merton, the Trappist monk who lived for twenty-seven years at the Abbey of Gethsemani, in New Haven, Kentucky, about two hours from Berea. Merton wrote prolifically on his continually evolving religious journey as well as on contemporary needs for social justice and ecumenism. His deep understanding of the contemplative life, shown in *Thoughts in Solitude* (1958/1999), and his engagement with the joys and challenges of writing (Inchausti, 2007) speak strongly to today's readers. Another text used in all the classes was Sarton's *Journal of a Solitude* (1992). A number of students connected with Sarton's frank discussion of her depression.

Contemplative writing students were urged to practice both *lectio* and *visio divina* in nature. Nature, along with scripture, has been considered a primary text of revelation (Paintner, 2012). Class visits by faculty in biology and desert ecology helped students deepen their understanding of ways to see and be in nature. "Sitting outside was just kind of listening to everything," one student said. Reading in the outdoors, a relatively human-free environment, allowed students to absorb words more richly. "Nature gives you a chance to be silent," another student commented. Exploring solitude—often a challenge for today's wired students—was another benefit of time in nature. "Contemplative writing helped me with the confidence to be alone," a student noted.

For other students, nature provided a larger, unstructured space in which to wander, physically and mentally. Two years after completing the contemplative writing course, one student recalled coupling his time reading outside with walking: "When you're in an environment that is so expansive, there is a chance that you make progress both physically and for me mentally," he said. "I am advancing my thoughts as I pass those same things."

Reading and seeing in nature helped students connect or reconnect not only with the larger universe but also with their deeper selves. One student found that reading Pablo Neruda's (2005) odes led him to realize the daily gratitude he had come to feel, particularly for the plants "that kept popping up over and over" in his life. He completed his independent writing project on gratitude for the many types of growing things that formed the heart of his study as a sustainability major.

For another student, rereading her own writing became a means of deeper interior discovery. Accidentally finding her contemplative writing journal months after the course's conclusion, she spent four hours rereading it. In addition to discovering a calmness and playfulness in her writing and sketching that was absent from her current, more intense art, she was reminded "to slow down and to remember what's important in my life." For another, contemplative reading and seeing became a means of entering an interior space, of centering in times of uncertainty: "Instead of not knowing what to do, I can just read and write and contemplate." Another student spoke of making photographs that were unplanned and private, as a means of centering (Jones, 2018).

Often the personal connection with text or image helped the student perceive beauty or strength amid difficult experiences. One student spoke of rereading a story of struggle, finding "beauty in things that are sad, that are in transition, . . . that you can't really grasp and keep." Another student made a photograph of a bird's nest on the shoulder of a garden statue of Jesus. Studying the image helped her to get beyond her anger at her church and to realize that she could find her own sense of higher power.

A third student had chosen the *Tao Te Ching* (Lao-tsu, 2006) as a spiritual reading. Following the course, he said that when he finds himself "submerged" by things flowing around him, he rereads the *Tao* to remind himself that he can persist: "I have always thought of everything as a river, that you have to let it push you but not push it back. Every time I read the Tao I think of that. . . . It shows me you can tolerate as things get worse and the currents get stronger."

As their individual practices of *lectio* and *visio divina* affected them, so students experienced benefits from having shared these practices. Each class made one or two retreats during the term to provide unstructured space and time to read, photograph or draw, write, and reflect alone and in community. Small groups of students often chose to get together outdoors to read aloud and comment on class or individually chosen texts or to draw or photograph together.

This creation of community was also evident in class discussions and in students' online journal writing. Students were required to make one journal post per week, but most posted several times, responding to different questions and to other students' responses.

In each class, small groups of students worked together to review one another's individual projects. This reading of one another's texts led to a deep exchange of ideas, many of which worked their ways into students' own projects. "It was like I fed off them," one student commented. Many recalled specific writings and art by classmates years after the class's conclusion.

Finding New Ways of Being, Creating, and Teaching

For many students, the introspection sparked by reading and seeing led to an openness to understanding the world in new ways, which in turn sparked creativity. One student, who had taken contemplative writing in her first year of college, designed a senior project arguing that a particular contemporary songwriter was creating accessible feminist texts. Listening repeatedly to the songs led her to explore new meanings and eventually feminist theory. This outward movement into a new discourse and worldview began with the "inwardness" and self-analysis she had done via contemplative writing texts. "What the class gave me was a space for introspection," she concluded.

Fear of the blank page can inhibit creativity, many writers find. Many contemplative writing students noted that the processes of contemplative reading and seeing impelled them to break silence, to create in words or images. After reading a passage, one student reported feeling, "Okay, you gotta write this." Another student developed his writing project through paralleling the journey taken by the Japanese poet Basho in *The Narrow Road to the Deep North* (1967). Like Basho, he said, "You'll see a flower and you'll just have to stop and write about it." And one student found himself drawn repeatedly to particular images in nature; he constructed a project that combined video and text.

Another element of reading and seeing that fueled students' writing was finding permission to integrate the personal and spiritual into academic writing. Reading Merton (1958/1999), one student noted, "made me more comfortable writing about the more spiritual, personal, and intangible." Studying Merton's photographs and writings about them ("A hidden wholeness," 2019) led students to see and express the mystery and significance residing in everyday objects (Jones, 2018).

Building on connections with texts and images led many students to create finished written and visual work, including poems, lyric essays, stories, photo essays, and artist's books. One student found that the ways the Sufi poet Rumi (2004) connected his feelings with his surroundings "really hit home." She created an important poem from the responses she had jotted down to various of Rumi's lines. More largely, this student found that her own "heavily emotional" writing evolved, via Rumi, into pieces where feeling was embedded in concrete aspects of her environment. For example, one of her project pieces arose from looking at the stones lining the path of the labyrinth she was walking. In her piece the labyrinth becomes "a place where you can come in with a lot of baggage you can leave when you go back out."

Students found that engaging in contemplative reading and seeing helped them to grasp not only the heart of a text or image but also its form. Basho's mixed form, known as *haibon*, gave permission for one student to create a project combining journal entries and poems. Many students chose to integrate visuals, whether photographs or sketches, into their written projects. Another student noted that "seeing the structure [in a reading] helps you to be a better writer." In particular, she found permission to approach poetry by reading a variety of poems in open rather than in traditional, rhymed form. Other students wrote about discovering visual form through an exercise in creating and using a cardboard frame (Jones, 2018; Zehr, 2005).

For several contemplative writing students, becoming a teacher has been another way of carrying forward work with contemplative reading and seeing. One key component is having become comfortable with silence as one delves into a text. One graduate, now teaching English to eleventh-graders, noted the importance of "wing time": waiting for his class to engage the big question he'd just posed. "It's so very very important," he said, "because they're learning the speaking and listening skills that are really useful." He coaches students to "remember that awkward silence is okay"—it means that minds are working, "and that's what we need to happen."

Another student, about to graduate and enter Teach for America, said that he had begun to study the ways people learn. His finding that not every person learns the same way would be a foundation of his teaching, he said. In particular, he hoped to make students aware that "going off to write in silence and solitude" is an approach they might try. "I hope to instill the love of writing in my students, and I think the key to that is options," he concluded.

Finally, the invitation embodied in *lectio* and *visio divina*—to read and see at one's own pace, level, needs, and desires—has allowed readers to discover or rediscover a joy in reading that is often lost in academe. "It's been a really long time since I read for fun," one student said. "I remember we got to go at our own pace a little bit. I remember just laying in bed and reading because I wanted to." An image from the first contemplative writing class's retreat in the Sonoran Desert outside Tucson, Arizona, speaks to the power of being absorbed in a book (Figure 5.1).

CLASSROOM PRACTICES TO FOSTER READING AND SEEING

Contemplative reading and seeing practices can benefit students in any liberal arts class (Barbezat & Bush, 2014; Gunnlaugson, Sarath, Scott, & Bai, 2014). The following teaching practices can be adapted for classes in humanities, social sciences, or natural sciences.

1. Begin each class with ten minutes of quiet time for reading, writing, and reflection. This period gives students a chance to clear their minds and bring their attention to the coming work. Miller and Hughes (2012) suggest ringing a bell to begin and end this time.
2. Allow choice among readings and viewings. Encourage students to choose among selections from a writer. Give options for students to choose additional texts relevant to their interests. When invited to choose, many students will take on texts or work with images that are more challenging than those typically selected for a class.
3. Invite students to lead written discussion of a particular week's readings. Students can extend their *lectio* and *visio divina* skills by posing written questions for classmates and responding to the responses. Posing a thoughtful question means engaging deeply in the assigned reading, letting it speak personally. For example, one student explored the idea that the "constant rush" of our lives causes us to "miss out on the beauty around us." He offered a passage from Rilke (1934/1993): "If

Reading the Word, the Self, the World 57

Figure 5.1. Jesse Wilhite, Berea '09, on retreat as part of contemplative writing class, Redemptorist Renewal Center, Cortaro, AZ, January 2009. *Photo by Libby Falk Jones.*

your everyday life seems poor to you, do not accuse it; accuse yourself, tell yourself you are not poet enough to summon up its riches" (p. 12). Then he invited classmates to connect this idea with the week's chapters in Zehr (2005). Lifting up a passage for contemplation invites other students to dwell there.
4. Ask students to keep a journal of responses to texts or images. Keeping a journal, in whatever form, provides an ideal place for listening to texts, experience, and thoughts. Journaling also results in a treasure trove of materials that can be mined and revised into finished writing.
5. Invite students periodically to reread their writings and review their visual creations. Rereading creates an occasion for additional *lectio* or *visio divina*. Reviewing one's own work is a means of self-observing and thus deepening self-knowledge, as well as of making additional connections to other texts, images, and ideas. One student noted that reviewing his journal had been the most productive element in keeping it. This habit of reflective self-observation is key to continued learning.

CONCLUSION

Lectio and *visio divina* can help students—and teachers—re-center their learning to become more open to discovery and connection. Students find that by slowing down their pace and attending more fully to the present—text or image—they are inhabiting a world much richer than they had realized. They discover as well that the skills of observing, pondering, reflecting, and responding are ways into that world, avenues of discovery now always available to them.

Through contemplative reading and seeing, students uncover the web of connections within themselves and among self, other, the natural world, and society. These practices help students enlarge their sense of self in the context of a textured, ever-amazing world. Teaching these practices becomes an opening experience as well, as the teacher stays present, open to what students bring forth. Such open, responsive teaching is at the heart of the writing classroom, and helping students engage *lectio* and *visio divina* is an important pedagogy for achieving this.

Further, students find that these reading and seeing practices provide an appropriate balance of discipline and freedom, key to lasting educational development. Being instructed to see is "a good instruction," one student noted. "Sometimes it opens you up to doing things you maybe wouldn't otherwise consider doing" (Jones, 2018). Contemplative reading and seeing reward patience, attentiveness, and time on task, qualities often absent in today's fragmented educational environments. Practicing *lectio* and *visio di-*

vina can lead to experiencing what Brother Paul Quenon (2018) calls "the gift of leisure" (p. 54). Such leisure, within today's busy, noisy world, is indeed a gift—and is necessary for cultivating an openness to possibility and a sense of larger unity with the universe.

ESSENTIAL IDEAS TO CONSIDER

- *Lectio* and *visio divina* provide a means for engaging in deep dialogue with a text or image—a dialogue that respects both the text/image and the sensibility the reader/seer brings to the experience.
- The processes of *lectio* and *visio divina* can be applied to materials in any field.
- Practicing *lectio* and *visio divina* can lead students to become more aware, to engage challenging ideas, to become more open to possibility, to develop confidence in their own capabilities, and to take joy in learning and creating.

REFERENCES

Barbezat, D. P., & Bush, M. (2014). *Contemplative practices in higher education: Powerful methods to transform teaching and learning*. San Francisco, CA: Jossey-Bass.

Chittister, J. (2011). *Illuminated life: Monastic wisdom for seekers of light*. Maryknoll, NY: Orbis Books.

Gunnlaugson, O., Sarath, E. W., Scott, C., & Bai, H. (Eds.). (2014). *Contemplative learning and inquiry across disciplines*. Albany, NY: State University of New York Press.

Hall, M. P., O'Hare, A., Santavicca, N., & Jones, L. F. (2015). The power of deep reading and mindful literacy: An innovative approach in contemporary education. *Innovación Educativa*, *15*, 49–60.

Hamma, R. M. (2002). *Earth's echo: Sacred encounters with nature*. Notre Dame, IN: Sorin Books.

"A hidden wholeness: The zen photography of Thomas Merton." Thomas Merton Center at Bellarmine University. http://www.merton.org/hiddenwholeness/. Retrieved 2 April 2019.

Inchausti, R. (2007). *Echoing silence: Thomas Merton on the vocation of writing*. Boston, MA: New Seeds/Shambhala.

Jones, L. F. (2018). Seeing mindfully: Fostering creativity and connection through contemplative photography. In M. Garbutt & N. Roenpagel (Eds.), *The mindful eye: Contemplative pedagogies in the visual arts* (pp. 21–38). Champaign, IL: Common Ground Research Networks.

Lao-tsu. (2006). *Tao te ching: A new English version*. (S. Mitchell, Trans.). New York, NY: HarperCollins.

Lichtmann, M. (2005). *The teacher's way: Teaching and the contemplative life*. Mahwah, NJ: Paulist.

Matsuo Basho. (1967). *The narrow road to the deep north and other travel sketches*. London: Penguin.

Merton, T. (1999). *Thoughts in solitude*. New York, NY: Farrar, Straus and Giroux. (Original work published 1958)

Miller, B., & Hughes, H. J. (2012). *The pen and the bell: Mindful writing in a busy world*. Boston, MA: Skinner House.

Neruda, P. (2005). *The poetry of Pablo Neruda*. (I. Stavans, Trans.). New York, NY: Macmillan.

Paintner, C. V. (2012). *Lectio divina: Transforming words and images into heart-centered prayer*. Woodstock, VT: Skylight Paths.

Quenon, P.O. C. S. O. (2018). *In praise of the useless life: A monk's memoir*. Notre Dame, IN: Ave Maria.

Rilke, R. M. (1993). *Letters to a young poet* (M. D. Herter, Trans.). New York, NY: Norton. (Original work published 1934.)

Rumi, J. (2004). *The essential Rumi* (C. Barks, Trans.). New York, NY: HarperCollins.

Sarton, M. (1992). *Journal of a solitude*. New York, NY: Norton.

Sher, G. (2002). *The intuitive writer: Listening to your own voice*. New York, NY: Penguin.

William of Saint Thierry (d. 1148). (1971). The golden epistle: A letter to the brethren at Mont Dieu 1.120-124. In Theodore Berkeley (Trans.), *The works of William of St. Thierry*, Cistercian Fathers 12 (pp. 51–52). Spencer, MA: Cistercian Publications. http://archive.osb.org/lectio/thierry.html.

Zehr, H. (2005). *The little book of contemplative photography: Seeing with wonder, respect, and humility*. Intercourse, PA: Good Books.

Chapter Six

Writing about Yoga

Lectio Divina *and the Awakening of the Soul*

Mary Keator,
Westfield State University

In his article "The Humanities and the Soul," John J. Conley (2015) states that the purpose of education is "to awaken [the students'] souls to deeper ways of being human" (p. 29). To awaken our souls is to become the subjects of our own learning, to experience what we are reading, reflect on it in the midst of our human condition, and allow these experiences to move us toward our full potential—the development of our whole person: body, mind, heart, and soul. The pedagogy exercised in the medieval monastic schools to awaken the students' souls to deeper ways of being human was called *lectio divina*.

In Writing about Yoga, the contemplative method of *lectio divina* from the Western monastic tradition was combined with the literature and practice of yoga from the Eastern tradition to help students learn about and come to understand the subject matter of yoga in order to write clearly about it; yet, in the process of learning yoga through the *lectio divina* method, the students began articulating in their writings their own self-discovery and holistic development.

Drawing from this monastic pedagogy of *lectio divina*, students in Writing about Yoga entered the world of the text as they engaged in the slow, focused, performative reading (*lectio*) of yogic texts and myths. Once within the world of the text, the students began to search it for deeper meaning (*meditatio*). As they discovered deeper meaning, they began to express their discoveries in integrated written responses (*oratio*), demonstrating their realizations and growing levels of understanding and transformation (*contemplatio*).

Each class began with establishing a tone of deep respect between the teacher and the students as all placed their hands together in front of their hearts, saying, "Namaste" (I bow to the light in you). As one student commented, this simple gesture led the students to deeper self-reflection:

> Most college courses I've taken so far aren't necessarily made for me as an individual. They tend to just be throwing out information in a general state. This class is completely different; it tends to be more self-reflective and has me more involved. For instance, the meaning of "Namaste" in our class. In the beginning, I was just kind of doing it because you demonstrated doing it and we did it too with you without a meaning really, but this past week I really focused on what you were saying about the meaning behind it. Namaste means "I bow to you" but we look in at ourselves and then look up and release it out to the world. While doing this I realized that it is a practice of self-awareness. By looking in at ourselves, we are evaluating who we truly are, our character, our values, our beliefs.

This gesture of honoring was followed by the class chanting the invocation to the *Katha Upanishad* together, a chant of commitment between the teacher and student to put forth effort to study the yogic texts peacefully together. Once the tone for the class was set, the students and teacher practiced yogic postures, meditated, read and dialogued about the readings, and reflected on their learning in their writing journals.

As the semester progressed, students continued to articulate their inner and outer transformation, using the adapted *lectio divina* method in Writing about Yoga. A male student, in his article, "Unexpected Lessons: How an Eagle and a Crippled Man Taught Me to Care," shared a pivotal, empowering moment.

> I began the semester with a lazy attitude. I simply wanted to hang out and basically do nothing. I was lethargic and apathetic. . . . I just did not care, especially about schoolwork. . . . I decided to care. I began to go inside myself, access my inner power and use it for good because of the influence of Garuda, the eagle. . . . Not only did I read the story, but each time we met in "Yoga and Writing" we would perform this pose (*Garudasana*). Slowly, something started to seep into me, and I began to embody the lessons of Garuda. I too had felt small. I felt disempowered and disconnected from my potential. . . . The story taught me that although our size makes us feel small, we have endless power inside us.

Through the practice of slow performative reading, the above student slowly began to enter into the world of the text and embody the qualities of Garuda. As he read and performed *garudasana* again and again during each class, "something started to seep into" him. Throughout the semester, he moved from a noncaring student to a caring student, from being "lazy," "lethargic," "apathetic," "small," "disempowered," and "disconnected" to a student who realized he had "endless power" within him.

Throughout the semester, the students read myths behind the various asanas (yoga postures), learned and practiced asanas, reflected on their meaning, and shared their experiences in their writings. Yet, as the students continued to enter into the contemplative space, read the texts, and perform the asanas together, something unexpected happened: They began to awaken to a deeper, fuller sense of self—hidden within—as they became more aware of the intricate connections and unity between their own body, mind, heart, and soul.

THE CONTEMPLATIVE SPACE

Before moving deeper into the pedagogy of *lectio divina* it is important to understand that contemplative pedagogy needs a contemplative space. In the monastic schools, *lectio divina* was practiced in a contemplative space. The Writing about Yoga classes met twice a week in the Albert and Amelia Ferst Interfaith Center on campus, which provided the students with a contemplative space, meaning, a quiet, clean and uncluttered space for their learning experience to unfold. Palmer (1993) wrote,

> Space may sound like a vague, poetic metaphor until we realize that it describes experiences of everyday life. We know what it means to be in a green and open field; we know what it means to be on a crowded rush-hour bus. On the crowded bus we lack space to breathe and think and be ourselves. But in an open field, we open up too; ideas and feelings arise within us; our knowledge comes out of hiding. (p. 70)

As Palmer notes, space matters. Yet it is often a challenge for contemplative educators to find such a space. The space itself was integral to the pedagogy and students noted the benefits, "The clear, inviting space allows me to be creative and work harder."

In addition, the support given by the director of the Interfaith Center, Fr. Warren J. Savage, was steadfast and invaluable. His generous offering of the space for the course, as well as his gentle presence with the students during the bi-weekly classes, contributed to the students' overall experience of feeling affirmed and welcomed. As Nouwen (1975) remarked, "When we look at teaching in terms of hospitality, we can say that the teacher is called upon to create for students a free and fearless space where mental and emotional development can take place" (p. 61).

At the beginning of each class, students entered the Interfaith Center, took off their shoes, moved the benches to either side of the room to open the space for class, and laid out their yoga mats in two rows facing one another. I also took off my shoes and laid out my mat in the front of the room, between the two rows, facing the students. As the semester progressed, the students realized the importance of preparing the space for their learning and practice.

At the end of the semester, I asked students to complete an anonymous questionnaire which asked the following question: Has practicing yoga in a contemplative space (the Interfaith Center), helped you become a better writer/supported your writing? (1) Not at all; (2) A little helpful; (3) Helpful; or (4) Very helpful. As you can see from the students' responses below, practicing yoga in a contemplative space had a profound impact on their learning. Forty-eight student responses are shown in Figure 6.1.

THE PEDAGOGY: *LECTIO DIVINA* METHOD

In Writing about Yoga, the ancient monastic practice of *lectio divina* was adapted to help students understand yoga in order to write intelligently and meaningfully about it. *Lectio divina* is a contemplative practice, composed of a fourfold movement (*lectio, meditatio, oratio,* and *contemplatio*). During the semester, the students learned how to read slowly and performatively, think critically, and respond meaningfully to what they read, experienced, and reflected.

Lectio, the first movement, teaches students to slowly read the text before them. For this course, the texts read included *Myths of the Asanas* (2010) by Alanna Kaivalya and Arjuna Van der Kooj as well as articles on yoga. Each reading corresponded to a specific yoga pose. As students slowly read about

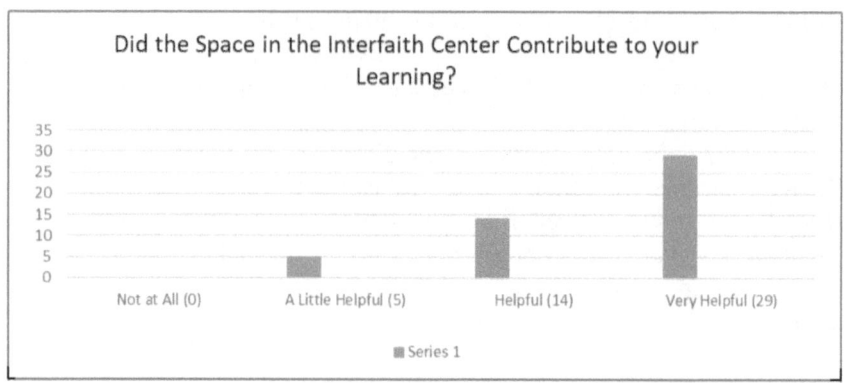

Figure 6.1. Did Space in the Interfaith Center Contribute to Your Learning?

the pose, they began to learn some basic information. For example, when the students slowly read the myth about *garudasana* (eagle pose), they learned the Sanskrit term. They also learned that the pose is named after Garuda, Vishnu's carrier, who first appeared "as radiant as a million suns." But his power frightened the gods; they "begged him to reduce himself in size and energy" (p. 97).

Next, students performed the pose—in this case *garudasana*—while repeating the name together out loud: "*garudasana.*" As Morson (2015) noted, "The real literary work is the readers' experience. This means the first thing a teacher needs to do is to help students have the experience the author is trying to create" (p. 25). No longer were students reading just with their eyes. As they performed *garudasana*, they were reading with their bodies, bones, and muscles and, in the process, began experiencing the affect that this way of reading had on their body, mind, heart, and soul. As one student commented, "Garudasana reminds us that we are powerful spiritual beings, even though we are in human bodies. I use that to remind myself of the spiritual power I have and let it help me meditate."

Meditatio, the second movement, teaches students how to search the text for deeper meaning. It consists of three main practices: rumination, memorization, and analysis. Through the practices of *meditatio* on *garudasana*, the students repeated the name of the pose along with its myth multiple times out loud throughout the semester. Slowly, the students began personally connecting to a deeper hidden meaning within the pose and began to have a subjective experience as they shifted their attention from the text back onto themselves: "The strength and power I feel while practicing these postures is unexplainable. Knowing that I have that kind of power in myself, makes me think, 'What else can I do?'"

One of the challenges educators face in adapting the *lectio divina* method in the classroom is how to incorporate the practice of *oratio*, the third movement. All too often, *oratio* is understood as prayer and is therefore seen strictly as a religious practice. However, *oratio* was the monk's response to time spent in *lectio* (reading) and *meditatio* (reflection and analysis). These responses took the form of spontaneous responses, liturgical celebrations, and extended reflections (Keator, 2018, p. 155–61).

Oratio is the students' meaningful responses to what they read, experienced, questioned, and reflected on. In Writing about Yoga, *oratio* (responses) took the form of spontaneous responses during class, weekly reflection papers, and even more formal written assignments, such as articles for the school newspaper, brochures, and newsletters for the campus counseling center. Students responded to their newfound understanding and experience of *garudasana* in various ways. For example, one student shared how she uses *garudasana* to focus on her homework:

> Garudasana is helpful for when you need to focus. The pose requires a lot of concentration so that you can balance. I use this pose when doing homework because I find myself getting distracted and side-tracked. By doing this pose, I am able to bring my mind back to my homework so that I can get it done right away.

Later in the semester, a male student connected this pose to his mental-emotional state:

> The eagle pose, also known as *garudasana*, reminds you that even though you feel small sometimes you are much larger than you think or feel. This was a helpful pose because when I would be feeling down about something or be mad at myself, I would remember I am a lot more than I am when I am at my lowest.

As one can see from the above responses, *oratio* (weekly reflection papers, class dialogue, formal written assignments) allowed students to articulate the affect these poses were having on them. Throughout the semester, students read, practiced, and reflected on the meanings within poses such as *tadasana* (mountain pose), *vrksasana* (tree pose), *garudasana* (eagle pose), *balasana* (child's pose), and *shavasana* (corpse pose). As they read, students learned about the stability and strength of a mountain, the generosity and flexibility of a tree, the inherent power of an eagle, the playfulness and wonder of a child, and the total surrender of a body. The *lectio* practice of slow performative reading also reinforced yogic terminology and helped students to learn and better understand what they were reading so that they could write authentically on their experience.

Contemplatio, the fourth movement, is the culmination and fruit of the *lectio divina* practice, which is the result of the practice. Through slow performative reading, deep reflection, and responses, students began to engage themselves holistically in their learning. They became active subjects, engaged holistically in self-exploration and self-discovery. No longer were the students passive recipients of information to memorize and regurgitate; instead, they became active learners, engaged in their learning and care for self.

THE RESULTS

Throughout the semester, the students continuously commented that the practice and teachings of yoga were helping them to understand the fullness of their being (body, mind, heart, and soul): "Stringing all different poses together helps the body and the mind and the soul." As they began reconnecting with themselves as whole persons, they flowed into a process of self-examination and began to write about and describe their inner worlds and the ways in which they began reordering them.

Body

Students shared how the practice of yoga was affecting their bodies. One student wrote about how *vrksasana* and *garudasana* strengthen her body:

> During the tree and eagle poses, I must balance on one foot as I tuck the other into my thigh and then wrap it around my leg. Continuing to practice these poses would allow me to strengthen my balancing skills which would really benefit me as an Irish step dancer.

The students began to see that yoga was "more than an exercise as it is used to connect and train your mind and body to work in unison." Students articulated in their writings that yoga was helping them to integrate their whole selves and feel healthy:

> Now it is interesting that I am starting to see the effects on my body and how continual practice makes my body healthy and fit. It is one thing to hear it be said and it's another to actually feel the effects of a healthy mind, body and soul for yourself.

Mind

The students also commented on the connection they began to experience between the body and mind: "My mind and body are starting to come together each class we have." They saw yoga as more than a physical exercise: "Yoga is more than an exercise as it is used to connect and train your mind and body to work in unison." They began to see yoga and meditation as a way to train and clear their minds:

> The new meditation we learned this week is definitely something I am going to use in my everyday life. Especially when I am having trouble falling asleep or just need to focus on my breathing for a minute. . . . This new one is way more soothing and it actually clears my mind. . . . I actually showed my boyfriend the new meditation method and he liked it a lot.

In addition, the students were learning self-acceptance:

> In my life, I have had a lot of difficulty. I was diagnosed with cancer in 2014. I had to undergo an operation, soon after I was diagnosed, in order to get rid of it. I was declared cancer free within a few months and have been ever since. Before and after having cancer, I have been in abusive relationships up until my current relationship. Because of all these things, I was diagnosed with depression and hyper anxiety. It has been a really difficult road to travel because of all these things, and yoga is one of the things that has really helped me. Through yoga I am able to focus my energy into improving myself and feeling better about myself. I am able to take all of the negativity and put it

outside myself. I am able to relax my mind and make myself the me I want to be, without being defined by my past and what I have been through. . . . I am able to change myself for the better.

Heart

Students also shared their inner emotional states as they wrote about self-love and self-acceptance:

> Self-love and self-acceptance have been two very big themes throughout these 3 weeks. I never really realized that I do not accept or love myself as much as I had thought.

In order to share this raw truth, the student must have had an experience that helped her to reflect and see that in the past she had not been loving and accepting of herself. Through their experiences with yoga, the students not only wanted to become more loving, but were developing techniques to help to do so:

> Learning to love all of yourself is one of the most important things to do, but it is also one of the hardest things to do. It's something I'm still learning to do. With the help of meditation, I have learned to focus and calm myself down easier. So, when my self-image gets out of control, I know how to bring my mind back to reality.

Soul

Again referring back to the wisdom spoken by Conley (2015), "The purpose of education is to awaken the soul to deeper ways of being human" (p. 29). Yet, today, the soul is hardly ever spoken about in terms of education. However, it is interesting that students wrote about the soul, spirituality, and grace:

> Now it is interesting that I am starting to see the effects on my body and how continual practice makes my body healthy and fit. It is one thing to hear it be said and it's another to actually feel the effects of a healthy mind, body and soul for yourself.

Students also commented on feeling a spiritual and graceful experience in *shavasana* (corpse pose):

> Today, we were introduced to something entirely new to me. Professor Keator brought in her harmonium and chanted with us and to us. I've never experienced something quite like that. It was beautiful. After the past couple of weeks, I have been forced to deal with a lot personally and taking time to stop and feel the vibrations was something I cannot quite explain. The crescendo

and decrescendos of the harmonium and Professor Keator's voice ran through my ears like crisp mountain water. As we laid in shavasana, I was almost brought to tears and my body was coated with goosebumps the whole time. The whole experience was very spiritual and graceful.

CONCLUSION

Throughout the semester, the adapted Western practice of *lectio divina* and the Eastern practice of yoga helped the students begin to see themselves as integrated whole persons (body, mind, heart, and soul), empowered to care for and love themselves. Instead of learning *about* yoga, the pedagogy of *lectio divina* helped the students to experience what they were reading in order to integrate their learning and write meaningfully about it. At the end of the semester, one student shared in her final reflection a lesson that will stay with her long after the course is over:

> When I leave this class, I know that each and every day throughout my life I can use what I learned. Each pose has revealed something that was hidden within me, new perspectives of myself came to light. Each pose contained a hidden message about what I lacked as a writer. I now know the importance of focus (vriksasana), voice (bhujangasana) and purpose (virabhadrasana). This class was built on the purpose of deepening my sense of self and shaped me into who I need to become as a writer. Looking down at my mat now, I see something different. It is no longer blank; rather, it is filled with stories of my semester's hard work; it is filled with my accomplishments.

ESSENTIAL IDEAS TO CONSIDER

- The original purpose of education was the formation and education of the whole student (body, mind, heart, and soul). How can educators reclaim this understanding and incorporate it into their pedagogy?
- *Lectio divina* is a viable pedagogical method in the formation and education of the whole student.
- Contemplative learning spaces, free of technological distractions, are an important component in the formation and education of the whole person. How can educators and administrators support the creation and use of contemplative spaces in education?

REFERENCES

Conley, J. J. (2015). The humanities and the soul. *America, 213*(9), 29.
Kaivalya, A., & Van der Kooj, A. (2010). *Myths of the asanas: The stories at the heart of the yoga tradition.* San Rafael, CA: Mandala.

Keator, M. (2018). *Lectio divina as contemplative pedagogy: Re-appropriating monastic practice for the humanities*. New York, NY: Routledge.
Morson, G. S. (2015). Why college kids are avoiding the study of literature. *Commentary*, *139*(7), 5.
Nouwen, H. (1975). *Reaching out: The three movements of the spiritual life*. New York, NY: Doubleday.
Palmer, P. (1993). *To know as we are known: Education as a spiritual journey*. New York, NY: HarperOne.

Chapter Seven

Lectio Divina as Contemplative, Anti-Oppressive Pedagogy in Social Justice Education Courses

Elizabeth Hope Dorman,
Fort Lewis College

The racial demographics of school-age children in public schools in the United States have been changing and continue to change. Euro-American white students are now in the minority; more than 50 percent of students enrolled in public schools now come from Hispanic, Asian/Pacific Islander, and other racial groups (National Center for Education Statistics, 2019). Additionally, more than 10 percent of US public school children identify as English language learners (National Center for Education Statistics, 2018a). In contrast, the vast majority of teachers in US public schools (80 percent) are white (Geiger, 2018). Thus, the racial gap is growing between most teachers and their students.

Additionally, a pernicious achievement or "opportunity gap" (Nieto & Bode, 2011) between whites and students of color remains (National Center for Education Statistics, 2018b). Given that most teachers are still Euro-American/white, while most school-age public school children now are students of color (with many being English language learners), these demographic shifts have strong implications for teacher preparation.

More than ever, in order to help close this so-called achievement gap, prospective and current teachers need to engage in experiences that prepare them to effectively teach culturally and linguistically diverse learners. Part of this is cultivating dispositions and habits that have the potential to further social justice and equity.

Teachers (both preservice and in-service) need to have opportunities to investigate and challenge their own conscious and unconscious biases, develop cultural awareness and responsiveness, and develop skills and dispositions for working with and responding to potentially uncomfortable and charged topics (Hammond, 2015; Landsman & Lewis, 2011; Nieto & Bode, 2011), including a willingness to be uncomfortable and "disturbed" (Wheatley, 2002). These characteristics are necessary for teaching in a culturally responsive, equity-oriented way (Hammond, 2015) and reflect aspects of anti-oppression pedagogy (Berila, 2016).

CONTEMPLATIVE, INTEGRATED, EMBODIED, CRITICAL APPROACHES TO ANTI-OPPRESSION PEDAGOGY

Contemplative practices such as *lectio divina* implemented in teacher education allow an integrated, embodied approach for learners to unwind the conditioned mental habits of racism, prejudice, white supremacy, colonization, microaggressions, and other forms of oppression that cause harm and suffering.

Contemplative practices invite learners to slow down, turn inward, and cultivate their inner landscapes as educators, while simultaneously developing content knowledge and skills for teaching. Through a range of approaches, such as breath and body awareness, beholding, *lectio divina*, meditation, mindful dialogue, journaling, silence, and the arts, the contemplative mind is opened and activated with the intention of cultivating awareness, concentration, and insight (Hart, 2000). In contemplative education, the process of learning involves integrating our interiority with our exterior identities, facilitating a more holistic experience of developing new understanding. This pedagogical approach can be applied in any course and facilitates meaning-making of content (Barbezat & Pingree, 2012).

One form of contemplative practice is *lectio divina*, a Benedictine exercise that is directly translated as "divine reading." Traditionally, monastics used the practice to study scripture with four specific movements. Contemporary applications of *lectio divina*, especially when used in learning contexts, typically involve four steps.

Lectio (reading) is the first step: Selecting, reading, and rereading a passage of text. As Dalton (2018) explains, the reader lets themself "be drawn to words that jump off the page, are illuminated, and feel significant in the moment, as if they were meant just for me" (p. 19). When *lectio divina* is conducted in groups, the facilitator often intentionally selects one common passage with which all participants will engage.

Meditatio (reflection) is the second step: In silence, the "words are allowed to simmer and ruminate in the embodied experience, letting them unfold and reveal insights" (Dalton, 2018, p. 19). Often this involves rereading the text several times, while feeling into the words and their meaning with all one's senses.

Oratio (response) is the third step: Traditionally, this stage involves individual praying. In contemporary, secular adaptations, the reader allows themself to respond to the text in whatever way feels appropriate. The idea is to tune into multimodal, holistic ways of knowing, and then to express a response in images or words (see Dalton, 2018).

Contemplatio (rest) is the fourth step: Dalton (2018) describes this as a receptive process of returning "to stillness, integrating the experience more deeply and allowing both the words and the images to touch the deepest parts, transforming me from within." This is a place for "embracing growing wholeness" (p. 20).

Dalton (2018) argues that *lectio divina* as a mindful, contemplative practice can contribute to a sense of balance and wholeness, and "is counter to the ... hurried pace of academic life" (p. 19).

Illustrated here is a modification of the classic *lectio divina* process applied in social justice education courses, along with how participants responded to the exercise. The details of how and why the *lectio divina* process was modified will be described subsequently.

Lectio divina in the context of social justice education allows for blending of contemplative inquiry and reflection (Zajonc, 2009) within an anti-oppression pedagogy framework (described below) that addresses the needs of diverse learners. It allows educators to connect the development of their inner selves with increased content understanding. This form of contemplative pedagogy can also strengthen students' ability to critically self-reflect (Barbezat & Bush, 2014) and remain present and embodied (Berila, 2016). These skills and dispositions support educators' effectiveness in culturally and linguistically diverse settings.

As Berila (2016) synthesizes, anti-oppression pedagogy blends together various specific approaches to social justice education and critical pedagogy (Freire, 1970) and is designed to "help students move toward being more integrated, whole, and compassionate beings" (Berila, p. 50). To achieve these aims, anti-oppression pedagogy reflects these principles and practices:

1. learning is politicized;
2. education systems are recognized as both sites of oppression and sites of resistance;
3. students are taught to apply the concepts to their everyday lives and the sociopolitical power dynamics with which they live;
4. objective "Truth" claims are challenged as forms of domination;
5. knowledge is instead understood as historically and culturally specific;
6. teachers and students participate in knowledge construction;

7. the process of learning is as important as the content of learning, if not more so;
8. democratic participation is highly valued;
9. awareness and consciousness-raising are critical;
10. multiple perspectives are highlighted, often centering the experiences of marginalized groups; and
11. students are encouraged to use their learning process to actively transform society in socially just ways. (Berila, 2016, pp. 11–12)

Berila's mindful anti-oppression pedagogy framework argues for the importance of an embodied approach to social justice education, going beyond learning about oppression at a conceptual level. She cites somatic expert Peter Levine's description of embodiment as a necessary component for "effectively transform[ing] both ourselves and the larger collective" (Berila, 2016, p. 33) in a holistic way:

> *Embodiment is about gaining, through the vehicle of awareness, the capacity to feel the ambient physical sensations of unfettered energy and aliveness as they pulse through our bodies.* It is here that mind and body, thought and feeling, psyche and spirit, are held together, welded in an undifferentiated unity of experience. (Levine, 2010, p. 279, emphasis in original, cited in Berila, p. 37)

Embodiment offers a path for educators to connect their inner lives and identities (interiority) with the outer circumstances (exteriority) of teaching students whose cultural backgrounds differ from theirs. Paying attention to and integrating one's reactions at the levels of mind, body, and spirit allow educators to respond from a place of groundedness and wholeness to discomfort, difficulty, and not knowing.

The *lectio divina* process described here, grounded in a social justice education text and course, reflects many different elements of anti-oppression pedagogy and allows students to practice embodied awareness that goes beyond intellectual understanding. Through contemplative practice that invites reflection and embodiment, educators are better able to stay in the present moment when faced with discomfort or difficulty and are more likely to become aware of their own multilayered biases and conditioned habits.

Berila (2016) further develops the idea of embodiment, especially in the context of anti-oppression work, with this passage:

> How do we know when we are happy, afraid, or angry? What does that feel like in our bodies? What sensations arise that we then characterize as particular states of being? What conceptual storylines do we attach to those sensations, and how can we tease apart our labeling of those bodily sensations from the tainting ideologies of oppression itself? (p. 42)

This description illustrates how embodied awareness can promote a sense of wholeness and integration in one's experience. Educators are more likely to respond from a place of nonreactivity to difficult or unfamiliar situations related to cultural difference if they are able to ground themselves in embodied, holistic awareness.

The *lectio divina* process described herein also illustrates aspects of Rendón's Sentipensante Pedagogy (2014), the name for which comes from combining "two Spanish words: *sentir*, which means to sense or feel, and *pensar*, to think" (p. 131). This approach is "based on wholeness . . . , respecting the harmonious rhythm between the outer experience of intellectualism and rational inquiry and the inner dimension of insight, emotion, and awareness" (p. 2).

Rendón (2014) argues that Sentipensante Pedagogy is a form of integrative learning in that "it represents the reunification of sensing and thinking to foster the acquisition of knowledge and wisdom" (p. 134). Importantly, this approach "also acknowledges the importance of dialogue and the shared construction of meaning" (p. 135).

Sentipensante Pedagogy also embodies several goals that specifically connect to Berila's anti-oppression pedagogy framework. An important aim of Rendón's approach is

> to disrupt and transform the entrenched belief system [. . .] about teaching and learning that acts against wholeness and appreciation of truth in all forms . . . [and which] divorce[s] the mind from the senses and separate[s] the learner from what is being studied. (2014, p. 135)

Another central goal of Sentipensante Pedagogy, drawing from the practice of co-constructed meaning, is to elicit "social awareness within the student and teacher and some form of social change in and out of the classroom" (p. 136). The modified *lectio divina* process described here appears to have helped participants move toward these aims.

The contemplative, integrated, embodied, critical pedagogical approaches described by Berila and Rendón also serve to disrupt the "apprenticeship of observation" (Borg, 2004; Lortie, 1975) that prospective educators likely developed as P–12 students, which typically leads to viewing learning as a passive exercise of receiving knowledge transmitted by an all-knowing teacher.

As preservice teachers experience the actively engaging elements of anti-oppression and Sentipensante Pedagogy through the *lectio divina* exercise, they develop mental models of teaching and learning that reflect contemporary, active views of learning (Bartolome, 2004). They will then be more likely to employ active, integrated pedagogy in their own classrooms.

CONTEXT

Presented here are the author's experiences of engaging preservice teachers in a modified *lectio divina* process in two separate social justice education classes at a southwestern US college where more than half of the students identify as people of color. This course is required toward teacher licensure. One section included twelve undergraduates, while the other class served twelve graduate students. The *lectio* process implemented was adapted from Oliver, Dalton, Hall, and Hoyser (2018).

The main inquiry question framing this study was: How did the students respond to this modified *lectio divina* process in alignment with its contemplative, anti-oppressive pedagogy aims? The primary data sources comprised the written reflections students completed after the in-class exercise, as well as the author's field notes and teaching reflections.

Modified *Lectio Divina* Process

Prior to the class meeting, students were assigned to read all of Chapter 8, "Bias in the Curriculum and in the Classroom," in the main course text, *Cultural Competence: A Primer*, by Jean Moule (2012). Moule's chapter is 25 pages long and includes the following subheadings, which provide a sense of the content: The Impact of Social and Racial Attitudes, Teacher Expectations Affect Student Learning, Cultural Aspects of Curriculum Delivery, Bias in Conceptualizing Ethnic Populations, Bias in Assessment, Bias in Literature, Bias in Textbooks, Curriculum Reform, Aspects of Curriculum Transformation, Child-Centeredness of the Curriculum, The Opportunity Gap, Social Action at Work, and two sections to help prospective teachers consider how to apply the chapter content concretely to their future classrooms.

The modified *lectio divina* exercise was introduced with the following instructions on a handout (presented in block quotes below for clarity) as well as orally. Students were guided through the process along the way, with the instructor helping them time each round and making sure they understood each set of instructions.

> There are four steps in the *lectio divina* process that are used in this classroom experience. Please document and then comment on your experience of each step. This can include how you experienced it and also the specific meaning(s) you uncovered in the shared aspects of the text:
>
> 1. *Lectio* (Reading)
> 2. *Meditatio* (Search for Meaning)
> 3. *Oratio* (Response)
> 4. *Contemplatio* (Insight and Wisdom)

Step-by-Step Process

> 1. *Lectio* (Reading): Become aware of a particular phrase, sentence, or short passage from the text that jumps out at you in some way. Listen to your intuition and your body's wisdom to guide you. Don't overthink this. It may help to consider passages that you want to argue with, agree with, aspire to, or analyze the assumptions behind. Once you have selected the passage, write it down in the note catcher along with page number. Then read aloud your passage to the group. The group's role is to listen attentively, listen with their minds and hearts open.

As noted above, students were assigned to read the chapter at home to prepare for class. This allowed them to read in a slow, mindful, embodied way and to pay attention to the intellectual, emotional, and physical responses they were having to the text. They were instructed to "listen to their bodies and hearts" and "feel into" the words and their meaning as they encountered the text while they were reading at home prior to class.

When they arrived to class, students were asked to look back through the chapter and select a certain passage that spoke to them in some way, without thinking too much about why. They were encouraged to use their body's wisdom and intuition as a guide, paying attention to sensations and emotions. This approach cultivates mindful embodiment, which Berila (2016) argues is crucially important for working with anti-oppression content.

Students chose their own passages from the chapter based on what spoke to them and felt most relevant and meaningful. This is different from a more traditional *lectio divina* approach in which the facilitator selects a common passage to which participants respond. However, with a wide spectrum of ages, racial identities, and life experiences represented in the classes (everything from 19-year-old sheltered white women from the homogenous suburbs to retired military leaders who had served combat in multiple wars), it was important for students to be able to choose the passage to focus on for the *lectio* exercise.

In class, students were put into small groups with three to five classmates. Students wrote down in the note catcher/graphic organizer the passage they had selected for this exercise from the chapter on bias in the curriculum and then took turns sharing aloud their passage with their small group. Classmates followed along in their copy of the book. Guidelines included allowing for silence and space in between each person's sharing and continuing to pay attention to responses and reactions they were having in their bodies and hearts to what their peers shared.

> 2. *Meditatio* (Search for Meaning): Reread the passage you chose, and pay attention intuitively to responses in your body, mind, and heart. Reflect again on the passage, searching for meaning that you can connect with or that you

> want to discuss. Notice any responses, thoughts, bodily reactions, emotions, connections that come to you. After engaging in this internal process of contemplative inquiry and reflection, please share your response with your group. The group's role is to listen attentively, listen with their minds and hearts open.

Per these instructions for the *meditatio* step, in class, students spent some time silently and slowly rereading and marinating in their selected passage from the chapter, leaning into the wisdom of their bodies, hearts, and intuition, as they listened for any other responses. After a period of silence, students were invited to share with their small group any additional noticings based on their internal listening process. The instructor guided the timing during this stage so that the groups were all able to experience silence simultaneously as they engaged in the *meditatio* stage.

Although not indicated in the original directions, most of the small groups did end up engaging in some open-ended response and reaction to one another after the period of silence. This felt natural and necessary and organic to me, even though it was not originally built into the process. But it seemed like an important part of the learning, so conversation was encouraged. Next time this process is implemented, even more interactive peer-to-peer discourse will be deliberately built in, rather than having individuals simply share their thoughts while being witnessed by peers.

> 3. *Oratio* (Response): Now, let your instincts/intuition guide you as you respond and connect yourself with the passage by creating a response. The response can be words, a short phrase, a drawing/sketch, a body movement or sound, etc.—whatever you feel most appropriately expresses your experience with the passage. After a few minutes, you will be invited to share your response with your group. The group's role is to listen attentively, listen with their minds and hearts open.

In this stage, a wide range of multimodal student responses to their selected passage from the chapter were represented. The majority of students chose an artistic response such as a sketch; quite a few drew diagrams. A few got up out of their chairs and presented physical, embodied responses. Passion permeated their responses.

Similar to after the *meditatio* step, students spontaneously provided some degree of oral response and reaction to one another's sharing. They truly seemed to feel moved to acknowledge one another. Even though this was not how the exercise had been conceived, it made sense as the process unfolded, and it seemed to deepen the students' engagement with and interest in the exercise. In future iterations of this modified *lectio divina* activity, structured, peer-to-peer interactive discourse will be deliberately built into the process directions and invited.

4. *Contemplatio* (Insight and Wisdom): Now, return to the text to reread your selected passage. Simply allow yourself to let the words land on you, take them in, experience them. Stay present during this process, with your body and mind in the same place at the same time. Just notice what it feels like to let the words land on you again. This is an internal process of personal discovery to uncover hidden biases and/or strengthen convictions, not something shared aloud with peers.

Similar to before they read the assigned chapter, students were encouraged to "listen to their bodies and hearts" and tune in to an embodied, "felt sense" of the meaning of their selected passage. This contemplative process invites a sense of wholeness as it was designed to help students get a sense of coming full circle with their selected passage and its emerging meanings.

Because the process described above in steps one through four took the allotted class time, students were asked to submit written responses to these prompts as homework:

Describe:

- what your initial response was to the passage you selected from Moule's Chapter 8;
- what you said to your small group after completing the *meditatio* process;
- what you created for your *oratio* response, and then tell a bit about it. (Please also submit your actual drawing or response.)

Then, respond to the following prompts as an overall reflection on the process:

- Drawing from this classroom activity, describe your own experience from the perspective as a learner who was a participant in the *lectio divina* process.

  - What was your overall response to it?
  - What about it, if anything, resonated with you? Explain.
  - What about it, if anything, was difficult for you? Explain.
  - Then, ponder and reflect on: How you might use and/or adapt a similar process in your future education work?

These reflections allowed students to engage in a metacognitive, contemplative inquiry on the value of the modified *lectio divina* process.

THEMES: STUDENT PERSPECTIVES ON *LECTIO DIVINA*

Deepened Understanding of the Text

Many of the students' written reflections noted that through this process of close reading and interacting with the text and their peers, connections were created across mind, body, and heart, and subsequently, their level of understanding of the actual words and their multidimensional meaning increased. Numerous student comments emphasized that the modified *lectio divina* process allowed them to "dig deeper." This comment characterizes what many communicated: "I knew that the passage meant something to me, but I had not really slowed down to think about why." Elaborating on this idea, another commented, "Reading something over and over internalizes every word and intensifies its overall meaning." And another noted that the process of going deeper with the text in this spiraling way helped them "become even more passionate about what the text says."

Interestingly, one student shared, "After searching for deeper meaning in this passage, I feel much more responsibility as a teacher. Even a simple statement to another teacher, assuming academic capabilities of other students, can affect those students throughout their entire lives." As another person described (with italics added by the author to clarify meaning),

> This assignment helped to create new layers of depth and understanding from excerpts of the chapter. I summarized the experience as passage [*actual words from the text*]—abstract thinking [*contemplative inquiry in meditatio phase*]—passage [*going back to the actual text and reencountering it*]—reflection [*meditatio, oratio and contemplatio phases*]. Through the process of thinking abstractly, I was able to step outside of the words which helped me contextualize the information. This allowed me to relate the content to myself.

Overall, students' responses indicated that this modified *lectio divina* process, which invited them to slow down and interact with and reencounter their selected passages multiple times and through a variety of modes (silently, aloud, with their bodies, via art or other nonlinguistic response), brought them to a more profound understanding than what they had initially interpreted. As the student above commented, it allowed them to "step outside of the words."

Their comments indicate that they created deeper meaning through connecting their initial conceptual reactions with their internal, embodied reactions to the content. What the students describe above is an example of Sentipensante Pedagogy, in which students' minds and senses are integrated, and the learner is less separate from what is being studied (Rendón, 2014).

Facilitated Emotional Literacy

Many students identified strong emotions that were evoked from the process of drilling down deep into their short, selected passage from the chapter on bias in the curriculum and classroom. Mapping their responses as a whole through multimodal approaches revealed a wide range of named emotions sparked by interacting with the text in a deepening spiral: anger, indignation, upset, shock, frustration, impatience, sadness, disappointment, confusion, as well as joy, inspiration, and motivation to act out in the world. As one student wrote in depth,

> During the *meditatio* process, I experienced the emotion of anger. Anger came up when I read in the chapter about how "teachers do not recognize the brilliance students possess, especially when students express themselves, evaluate a problem, or address a situation in a way unlike the teacher . . ." (Moule, 2012, p. 180) because I thought about how teachers need to be open-minded.
>
> When I read, "a teacher's decision to lower their expectations are made visible through all forms of explicit, implicit and null curriculum" (Moule, 2012, p. 180), I felt the emotions of passion and anger mixed together. I also felt frustration. My thoughts surrounded the idea that teachers need to do the *exact opposite* of what this passage is saying and because level of expectation makes such a huge impact, that teachers need to be acutely aware of this.

One student described feeling supported by "the attention put in to listening. Not just listening to your group members, but the intention and time allowed to listen to yourself about what you read." As another wrote, "Meditating on certain passages that resonated with me worked well for me because I do like looking inward to see *why* I believe in the ideas I have."

This internal listening and inquiry process, which involves paying attention to one's embodied responses and blending together what one *thinks* with what one *feels* (in the style of Sentipensante Pedagogy), appears to have allowed participants to create a sense of wholeness by integrating their conceptual and emotional reactions.

Helped with Understanding Past Experiences

Quite a few students expressed that slowing down and interacting so deeply with one passage sparked deeper understanding of past experiences from their lives. As one student who felt rather shut down in high school by her teachers elaborated,

> While I was thinking about that phrase, I came up with a question about my past. Would it have made a difference if my school had tried to encourage us, the students, to raise our voices and show our potential through it? Would we have tried to make some changes in the school culture? If I would have had that opportunity, would I be different now?
>
> I believe that my peers and I would have tried to make some changes in the school culture and would have developed a more powerful potential. In my case, since I grew up being shy, I would probably have a stronger personality now if I would have had those opportunities in school.

And another student commented,

> During the *meditatio* process, I thought about my past experiences at my high school, especially with regards to my best friend Martin. I do truly believe that he was able to graduate because there was someone in his life—myself and my family—who held him to high expectations where no one else would. In the end, he graduated, and he's doing alright and is caring for his brothers now, who unfortunately did not graduate high school.

Teachers certainly draw from their past experiences as they construct their professional identities. This modified *lectio divina* process appears to have helped some of these students get perspective on situations from their personal histories that could have an impact on how they approach their work and their role as educators. The process of slowing down, cultivating various forms of awareness, and co-constructing integrated understanding through sharing and dialogue with their peers appears to have led some students to new insights about past experiences, which form part of their identities.

Inspiration to Take Social Action, Work toward Equity

Some of the participants expressed feeling particularly inspired to act in a way that fosters social justice and equity after the *lectio divina* process. Describing what she created during the *oratio* step, one student wrote,

> I drew a picture of a student with a giant hammer. The student smashes the school-to-prison-pipeline while exclaiming, "I matter!" The idea flowed from my feelings about my brother and students like him. Schools unwittingly teach these kids that they are criminals, that they have no value. I feel like if I can see value in each student and show them how to see the same, then my students will be less likely to end up in the loop of poverty and criminalization.

Another student expressed that the process of spiraling down into levels of meaning within the selected passage

> made me realize about the youth voices in the school and the power those could have. We, as educators, should encourage our students to raise their voices, to let the world hear their beliefs, their feelings, their thoughts, their ideas. Giving the children that opportunity would probably generate more academic engagement and a deeper connection with the school, as they would feel important by having their voices heard.

A prospective teacher who had recently watched a TV special on the Vietnam War drew from that experience to create a comparative analogy for his *oratio* response:

> I drew the flag of North Vietnam, representing the regular army, compared to the flag of the Viet Cong, representing a guerrilla army. My thinking was that combatting conscious bias takes on a very different form than combatting

subconscious bias. Where conscious bias is overt and easy to recognize, much like a regular army, subconscious bias takes on many forms and is harder to define, much like a guerrilla army. The main idea is that we have to be creative and willing to adapt to address and correct subconscious bias.

These excerpts illustrate some of the ways in which the modified *lectio divina* process elicited an awareness that blends sensing and thinking, along with both internal and social awareness among participants (Rendón, 2014). It also inspired prospective teachers to apply the concepts to their classrooms and everyday lives, and to "use their learning process to actively transform society in socially just ways," as Berila (2016, p. 12) encourages in her anti-oppression pedagogy framework.

CONCLUSION

This particular adaptation of *lectio divina* contained multiple layers of learning for the participants through the lens of contemplative anti-oppressive pedagogy. The book chapter on bias in the curriculum and classroom that they read for this exercise is also explicitly grounded in an anti-oppression framework.

Additionally, this version of *lectio divina* itself provided opportunities for students to experientially participate in multiple elements of anti-oppression, Sentipensante Pedagogy (Berila, 2016; Rendón, 2014). For example, sparked by the chapter content and their blended sensing-thinking responses, students constructed knowledge in collaboration with their peers. They had the opportunity to contemplate and cultivate multiple perspectives about the chapter content. Their integrated mind-body-heart responses allowed them to raise consciousness about important social justice issues.

Furthermore, participants were encouraged to think about how to adapt and apply this *lectio divina* exercise to their own future classrooms. As such, it provided an opportunity to consider how to implement aspects of anti-oppression pedagogy in their own future work as P–12 teachers.

Lectio divina is a powerful way for learners to make relevant connections between texts and themselves. This works particularly well with content—such as social justice education and anti-oppression pedagogy—that evokes strong emotions and potential controversy. The process can build students' embodied awareness, emotional intelligence, and deep cognitive understanding simultaneously, reflecting both Sentipensante Pedagogy and Berila's anti-oppression pedagogy framework.

This contemplative exercise also allows students to examine their assumptions, values, beliefs (Bartolome, 2004), which must be done in order for their own pedagogy to serve students from culturally and linguistically diverse backgrounds and contribute to closing the achievement or "opportunity gap."

ESSENTIAL IDEAS TO CONSIDER

This modified *lectio divina* process:

- is a simple, interactive exercise to assist students in simultaneously meeting academic goals and developing their inner awareness. Social awareness is also developed when this is structured as a small group collaborative learning activity;
- deepens participants' understanding of texts and of themselves;
- can be applied to any content area, and prompts can be adjusted for developmental level of learners;
- illustrates an example of anti-oppression pedagogy, as it allows participants to generate multimodal knowledge and meaning in collaboration, cultivates multiple perspectives, and encourages mindful embodiment; and
- provides the opportunity for participants to encounter and reencounter concepts in a slow, mindful, embodied way that allows for processing of complex, rich, potentially challenging, and/or controversial content.

REFERENCES

Barbezat, D., & Bush, M. (2014). *Contemplative practice in higher education*. San Francisco, CA: Jossey-Bass.

Barbezat, D. P., & Pingree, A. (2012). Contemplative pedagogy: The special role of teaching and learning centers. In J. E. Groccia & L. Cruz (Eds.), *To improve the academy: A journal of educational development*, 31 (pp. 177–91). San Francisco, CA: Jossey-Bass. https://doi.org/10.1002/j.2334-4822.2012.tb00681.x.

Berila, B. (2016). *Integrating mindfulness into anti-oppression pedagogy: Social justice in higher education*. New York, NY: Routledge.

Bartolome, L. I. (2004, winter). Critical pedagogy and teacher education. *Teacher Education Quarterly*, 97–122.

Borg, M. (2004). The apprenticeship of observation. *ELT Journal*, 58(3), 274–76.

Dalton, J. E. (2018). Embracing a contemplative life: Art and teaching as a journey of transformation. In J. E. Dalton, E. H. Dorman, & K. Byrnes (Eds.), *The teaching self: Contemplative practices, pedagogy, and research in education* (pp. 13–25). Lanham, MD: Rowman & Littlefield.

Freire, P. (1970). *Pedagogy of the oppressed*. New York, NY: Herder and Herder.

Geiger, A. (2018, August). *America's public school teachers are far less racially and ethnically diverse than their students*. Pew Research Fact Tank. Retrieved from http://www.pewresearch.org/fact-tank/2018/08/27/americas-public-school-teachers-are-far-less-racially-and-ethnically-diverse-than-their-students/.

Hammond, Z. (2015). *Culturally responsive teaching and the brain: Promoting authentic engagement and rigor among culturally and linguistically diverse students*. Thousand Oaks, CA: Sage.

Hart, T. (2000). From information to transformation: What the mystics and sages tell us education can be. *Encounter: Education for Meaning and Social Justice, 13*(3), 14–29.
Landsman, J., & Lewis, C. (2011). *White teachers, diverse classrooms.* Sterling, VA: Stylus.
Levine, P. (2010). *In an unspoken voice: How the body releases trauma and restores goodness.* Berkeley, CA: North Atlantic Books.
Lortie, D. (1975). *Schoolteacher: A sociological study.* Chicago, IL: University of Chicago Press.
Moule, J. (2012). *Cultural competence: A primer for educators* (2nd ed.). Boston, MA: Cengage.
National Center for Education Statistics (2018a). *The condition of education: English language learners in public schools.* Retrieved from https://nces.ed.gov/programs/coe/indicator_cgf.asp.
National Center for Education Statistics (2018b). *The condition of education.* Washington, DC: US Department of Education. Retrieved from https://nces.ed.gov/pubs2018/2018144. pdf.
National Center for Education Statistics (2019). *Status and trends in the education of racial and ethnic groups. Indicator 6: Elementary and secondary enrollment.* Retrieved from https://nces.ed.gov/programs/raceindicators/indicator_rbb.asp.
Nieto, S., & Bode, P. (2011). *Affirming diversity: The sociopolitical context of multicultural education* (6th ed.). New York, NY: Pearson.
Oliver, K., Dalton, J., Hall, M., & Hoyser, C. (2018, October). *Reimagining community & scholarship: Lectio divina as a tool for transformative education.* Presentation at the 10th Annual Conference of the Association for Contemplative Mind in Higher Education, Amherst, MA.
Rendón, L. I. (2014). *Sentipensante (sensing/thinking) pedagogy: Educating for wholeness, social justice and liberation.* Sterling, VA: Stylus.
Wheatley, M. J. (2002). *Turning to one another.* Berkeley, CA: Group West.
Zajonc, A. (2009). *Meditation as contemplative inquiry.* Herndon, VA: Lindisfarne Books.

Chapter Eight

Embodied Justice

We Are the Divine Text

Vajra M. Watson,
University of California, Davis

Throughout history, poets have served a sacred role as storyteller, teacher, and communicator. In many societies, these lyrical artists are heralded as cultural keepers and soul shakers. Consider for a moment the legacy of literary arts in West African Griot traditions, the clout of poetry in Somalia, the innovative, South Bronx street-based literacies that grew into hip-hop, and the contemporary youth spoken word performance poetry movement thriving from Sacramento to Soweto.

Unfortunately, within this ancient legacy of transformative praxis, there have been interruptions and injuries. Inside modern industrial classrooms, the literary arts were placed inside a literature canon where they were suffocated from the pulse of recitation and innovation. It is no surprise that far too often the word *poetry* conjures up images of dead white men. This erasure colonizes poetry and moves it away from its original nature and nexus of power.

In response to the larger colonization of learning, Greene (2009) explained that "of course we want to empower the young for meaningful work . . . but the world we inhabit is palpably deficient: there are unwarranted inequities, shattered communities, unfulfilled lives." So, she asks, "How are we to move the young to break with the given, the taken-for-granted—to move towards what might be, what is not yet?" (p. 84). To answer Greene's question, poetry provides a unique platform to play with words and picture alternative futures.

Between what is and what could be, there is poetry.

Exploring this sacred connection between pedagogy and possibility occurs in the teaching of spoken word performance poetry through the lens of *lectio divina*—divine reading. This investigation is guided by an overarching question: How do we educate the whole person in ways that nurtures personal transformation and collective belonging?

To answer this query, the research context will be provided followed by three core concepts in the literature that frame the analysis: research on spoken word performance poetry, the connections between art and activism, and the spiritual practice of slowing down to become more fully present. How these ideas are enacted and embodied will then be demonstrated inside disparate spaces—from continuation schools to juvenile hall facilities, from urban high schools to university lecture halls, from junior high school kids to professional development trainings for adults. Irrespective of the environment, these findings suggest that as we deeply and divinely read each other's words, we enact what I call *rituals of awakening*.

RESEARCH CONTEXT

Sacramento Area Youth Speaks (SAYS) was founded in 2008 as an innovative critical literacy and teacher professional development organization designed to engage underperforming youth of color and educators in Sacramento, California. With hip-hop and spoken word performance poetry at its core, SAYS community-based poet-mentor educators work inside middle and high schools to provide culturally relevant instruction to predominately Black, Latinx, and Southeast Asian students via workshops, courses, mentoring, the citywide SAYS Poetry Slam competition, and a large youth conference that takes place at the University of California, Davis.

Over the last decade, SAYS has developed an award-winning youth empowerment model that connects the hood and higher education. SAYS has also created employment pathways for former SAYS students to become poet-mentor educators and teaching artists. In this capacity, they complete a rigorous training that focuses on critical pedagogy, social justice instructional strategies, and the literary arts. Subsequently, they work in schools and community spaces to reach and teach the next generation of artists, activists, and academics (Watson, 2013, 2016). For information and videos on SAYS, visit says.ucdavis.edu.

Inside various SAYS spaces—whether in the community, the university, or the schoolhouse—participants engage in intensive writing workshops and subsequently share their work during community circles. The sharing circles are highly personal, and many times the participants have to hold space for one another to heal (Watson, 2017). Haddix (2013) describes this act of critical engagement as "listening face-to-face" and "eye-to-eye." The SAYS vision of embodied learning is for each person in the room to be fully seen and deeply heard as an active member of the whole—a concept that will be contextualized through the literature and elucidated in the findings.

POETRY FOR THE PEOPLE

Writing can embody its own birthing process. As a practice of insight, what is believed starts to get conceived. As poets, this happens upon the page. And then through the sharing process—literary performance—artists publicly give birth to their words; now their ideas live outside of the self in/of community with the wider world. This communal process of sharing one's story has pedagogical implications.

Freire asserts that "[h]uman beings are not built in silence, but in word, in work, in action-reflection" (1993, p. 28). In poetic writing workshops, the prompts are personal (e.g., *When I look in the mirror I see*; *I am not who you think I am*), guiding participants to expose themselves to themselves. Often, during the freewriting response time, everyone sits in a circle and writes side-by-side; each person is encouraged to let go of the rational thought and forgo the technicality, skill, and product and instead intuitively dance with their own voice, play with words, and experience limitless creative expression.

For Lorde (1984), the practice of poetic creation is rooted in Black feminist theory. In *Sister Outsider*, she explains that within each person there is a dark, ancient, deep reserve of emotional power. She urges us to "respect those hidden sources of our power" and to "train ourselves to respect our feelings, and to discipline (transpose) them into a language that matches those feelings so they can be shared." She then urges us to use words not only to contemplate reality, but also to reimagine it. She continues, "And where that language does not yet exist, it is our poetry which helps to fashion it. Poetry is not only dream or vision, it is the skeleton architecture of our lives." This kind of *poetry for the people* is distinct and disruptive: "I speak here of poetry as the revelation or distillation of experience, not the sterile word play that, too often, the white fathers distorted the word poetry to mean—in order to cover their desperate wish for imagination without insight" (pp. 36–37). In teaching poetry, it is important to acknowledge its orientation toward resistance and understand its roots.

Building on Black poetic traditions, spoken word performance poetry and hip-hop pedagogies have expanded into a worldwide phenomenon—especially within youth culture. The literature base has also been growing rapidly. In the last two decades, empirical studies on spoken word and hip-hop have burgeoned (e.g., Akom, 2009; Emdin, 2016; Fisher, 2005, 2007; Hill, 2010;bJocson, 2008; Love; 2012; Rose, 1994; Watson, 2016; Weinstein, 2018; Weiss & Herndon, 2001). A number of these studies focus on how adults and youth work together to create physical, intellectual, cultural, and emotional spaces where each participant may "insist upon [their] right to exist and declare [their] divinity" (Moon, 2014, n.p.).

Spoken word poetry is written for community; the intended publication is on stage in front of a live audience. This contrasts with the *literary* or *academic* or *page* poem, which is written primarily to be read on the page in isolation. Defining different kinds of poetry purely by their mode of operandi can be problematic; however, for some, spoken word's poetic difference is located in its ideological orientation, described as a democratic approach to aesthetics and public pedagogy (Ensley, 2015; Hill, 2010; Stanton & Tinguely, 2001). In this approach, artistic excellence is decentered in favor of participation in an experience that encourages radical vulnerability, truth-telling, and courageous encounters.

A growing number of scholars are examining the ways multimodal literacies are holistic and embodied (e.g., Enriquez, 2016; Schmidt & Beucher, 2018; Yagelski, 2009). This is especially true in a poetry slam competition. Here's a basic example of this unique literary extravaganza.

Generations of people from various backgrounds gather together at the local Opera House for the Youth Poetry Slam Finals. The event is sold out. Participants watch, snap, stomp, and applaud as middle and high school youth share stories, give testimony, and recite their lives on the mic. Each poet has only three minutes and twenty seconds to proclaim his or her piece to the world. Often, the short time span belies the depth of expression. These students have learned various writing and performance techniques (using minimal words to have a maximum impact); they have completed intense editing to reach this moment—when the poem is ready to share publicly. Their artistic mastery is often mesmerizing.

Prior to this penultimate moment on stage, there are important pedagogical implications of this literary arts movement that deserve exploration. At SAYS, we encourage students to become the authors of their own lives and agents of change. Our stories are not just for ourselves but can serve a wider purpose. There is strength in struggle, power inside pain, and even our existence embodies a form of resistance. The poem is teacher and student; art and activism.

ARTIVISM

Sandoval and Latorre (2008) define *artivism* as a "hybrid neologism that signified work created by individuals who see the organic relationship between art and activism" (p. 82). They posit that for Chicanx youth, artivism is often deployed as a means to transform themselves and their communities. Dalton (2018) echoes this sentiment: "Art is a change agent" (p. 16).

Historically, marginalized populations have leveraged poetry as a genre and method to articulate their politics, and often to dissent, on their own cultural terms. Faulkner (2009) argues that poetry often pays attention to the "particulars" of embodied knowledge, providing insight into ideologies of new realities. Furthermore, women and youth have utilized poetry within social movements where they have been silenced. Clark (2004) and Hope (2018) posit that Black and Asian American women and youth in the 1960s were major poets of the period as they often used poetry as a form of activism.

The SAYS poet-mentor educator Denisha "Coco Blossom" Bland has a similar outlook on artivism and defines it as "using your art to do better for your community. . . . I actually learned it over the years, but just political art." She explains:

> I always have that on my mind every time I sit down to write a poem that's like one of the first things I think about: Is this poem for me first? Is it something I just need to write and put in my book? Or is this a poem finna be something that I need to give to the people . . . SAYS actually helped me learn that.

Speaking truth to power is at the core of the art of spoken word poetry and performance. Armed with nothing more than a microphone, spoken word artists have been disrupting the status quo, confronting injustice, and advancing critical engagement within communities, campuses, and the world. My research follows the disruptive oral genealogies developed and imaginatively explored by poets and performers of color such as Amiri Baraka, Audre Lorde, June Jordan, Kendrick Lamar, Mahogany Brown, Sunni Patterson, Tupac Shakur, and Nikki Giovanni, to name just a few.

It is important to acknowledge that the next generation of artivists are in our classrooms, *now*. They desperately need platforms that illuminate and celebrate who they are becoming.

The German poet and playwright Bertoldt Brecht (2015) once said in an interview about his poetry, "You can't write poems about the trees when the woods are full of policemen" (p. 7). Although Brecht was from a different place and time, his account is an accurate reflection of a "reality pedagogy" that strives to meet students where they are (Emdin, 2016). Poetry is not always pretty and that is because it is meant to be truthful.

Consider for a moment the poem written by a young teenager, the now iconic Tupac Amaru Shakur, whose poem "Did you hear about the rose that grew from a crack in the concrete" (2006) exposes the immense strength and fortitude needed to overcome structural oppression and the material forces that constrain life and one's ability to grow. In his writing, he further explains: "You see you wouldn't ask why the rose that grew from the concrete had damaged petals. On the contrary, we would all celebrate its tenacity. We would all love its will to reach the sun. Well, we are the roses. This is the concrete. And these are my damaged petals" (p. 3).

As life becomes primary text, the poem serves as an extension of the person. Liberating literacies is quintessentially about the poem. Not poem as rarefied object, but poem as revealer and healer; poem as movement maker.

This form of artivism demands action. Yet in the realm of community organizing and the urgency to fight injustices, the work itself can become heavy. Slowing down might even feel selfish amid the immediacy of inequities, police brutalities, and constant emergencies. So we run and run and often barely catch our breath. Yet justice—literally and figuratively—demands balance. Thus a transformative praxis does not live just in our heads, but also in our hearts—and most definitely in our hands and feet. In other words, it is not merely what is conceived that is revolutionary, but what is achieved, daily, in how we are *living justice*. Thus liberation becomes the poetry of our lives.

P...A...U...S...E

There is a popular slogan in community organizing work: "Pause for the cause." This is an important pedagogical concept. In 1968 Merton discussed the "innate violence" of being too busy with the "rush and pressure of modern life" (p. 81). Dalton (2018) extends this idea when she writes, "Ignoring my body and my heart, I force personal will to complete my 'to do' tasks, despite signs of fatigue or stress. I become oriented toward goals and making things happen, pushing against the very loud messages I receive to pause" (p. 21). Professional busyness can serve as a distraction from areas of our life and parts of our self that need attention, perhaps even healing.

Moving from the personal to the political, slowing down connects to decolonial practices—consciously reorienting oneself in relation to space and time (Patel, 2016). Pausing can serve as a productive interruption to competitive ways of being, doing, and knowing.

So then, where is the pedagogy that embraces the pause? One possible answer is *lectio divina* reading. Dalton (2018) writes, "The process of reading slowly, savoring and allowing words to be 'felt' or embodied, is counter to the pace of academia where the emphasis often requires grasping new ideas and concepts, oftentimes superficially skimming literature" (p. 18). As explored throughout this book, *lectio divina* is a ritual that reorients time and space, and more importantly, shape-shifts the space between us. As we draw closer toward one another—in this case, through poetry—classrooms become fertile ground for the creation of beloved communities.

WE ARE THE DIVINE TEXT

There is a fast-paced nature to life, and this often spills into SAYS spaces. Participants enter into the classroom quickly and loudly, distracted by their phones and competing activities. This is not merely about young people; adults can be just as difficult to engage in a process of slowing down.

To counteract this pace, today, all the chairs are in a circle. Two dozen tenth grade students from Grant Union High School in Del Paso Heights (D.P.H.) shuffle into class and grab their journals from the box labeled "5th period." On the whiteboard, the following statement is written:

> Come In
> Place Your Notebook
> And Pen/cil
> Under Your Chair
> Sit Still
> And talk to the person sitting closest to you.
> Ask them . . .
> Who are you grateful for and why?
> *(Take turns answering this question. You have 3 minutes each.)*

Following this conversational warm-up, students transition to focus on the activity. Through call-and-response, we first review our intentions:

As we grow as learners, we will read ourselves, one another, and this world anew. Throughout this process,

- *We commit to practicing freedom.*
- *We strive towards radical vulnerability.*
- *We represent personal and collective accountability.*
- *We recognize that our full presence inspires our full humanity.*
- *We will hold each other's words, hear each other completely, and will heal holistically.*

Today we are going to read a *I am from* poem that one of our classmates just submitted the other day. Denise is a student in this class; she is sitting amongst her peers within the circle and she gave me permission to share it. We only have one copy of her poem for the entire class to share. Let's begin our reading ritual.

We go around in a circle, passing the paper; each student reading one line at a time. I set my phone alarm for thirty seconds; the sound of chimes will bring our focus back together.

We enter into a moment of silence.

The chimes ring. So we go around the circle again, but this time when each student reads a line, we all repeat the line. This form of call-and-response fills the classroom with the voices of the students who are repeating each stanza in unison.

We enter into a moment of silence.
I ask the class which line speaks to them and/or their lived experience.
Students explain what aspect of the poem moves them and why.
We enter into a moment of silence.
One student is selected to read the entire poem to the group. If the author of the poem happens to be in the class, they will be the one to read it out loud to everyone else.
We take a final moment of silence.
To close the ritual, we go around in a circle with each student reading one line at a time (similar to what we did in the opening).

Below is the poem we are reading through the pausing and reflecting ritual of *lectio divina*:

D.P.H.

I am from a large crowd that is not all the same.

I am from the thud of a body drop after a bullet hits throw [through] a little black boy's brain.

I am from whips, chains and physical strains that my ancestors had to go throw [through] so that my people to remain.

I am from D.P.H.

The deepest part of hell and the name reminds me of the closing doors of a cell.

I am from the thug life looking for a savior.

The demons on my block because the devil is my neighbor.

I am from the quarter that drops into a hobo's cup or the greedy eyes that look at them like their shit out of luck.

I am from the long long lines of soup kitchen where people fights just to eat.

I am from scattered tears on abused child feet.

I am from a song by R. Kelly called I wish I wish I wish and I hope the lyrics come true as I wish myself out of this pit.

I am from a place where fear and hate concurs [conquers] our dreams.

There you will find what poverty truly means.

I am from a place with lost love where everybody seems to lose faith in you even the God above.

I am from a place where the words hope and pray are only used when you have to go to court trial the next day.

I wish that I could have made this poem a little sweeter before I begun.
But sadly it's just not sugar coated where Im from.

Through our reflection exercise, Denise shares with us that she needed an outlet for her anger; instead of having to fight, she learned how to write. Building on this sentiment, I direct the class to take out their notebooks and write a letter to poverty.
Dear poverty...
After four minutes, the students are told to put their pens and pencils down and take a deep breath. Stretch a bit. Tell a person near them, "Thank you for coming to class today. We needed you here."
And we begin again. I offer them the next prompt.

What is your response to this quote by Bryan Stevenson (2014) in Just Mercy*:*
"The opposite of poverty is not wealth, the opposite of poverty is justice."

Students sit writing with music playing lightly in the background. Five minutes before the bell rings, we specifically thank Denise for sharing and inspiring us. We collectively acknowledge her radical vulnerability that opened us for deeper reading and more radical writing. Notebooks are placed back into the bin and students leave class.

Now, from a pedagogical standpoint, what just happened during this fifth-period English class at a large urban high school? A divine reading process was used as an embodied and liberatory practice. This was an adaptation of *lectio divina*, which was originally designed for sacred reading of scripture. Through the *lectio divina* process, reading is made communal. The reader repeats words and practices forms of meditation with the text such that he or she is able to listen through the ear of the heart. As a way to enact mindful literacy, *lectio divina* "can inspire in us a reverence for word and thing and for one another" (Hall, O'Hare, Santavicca, & Jones, 2015, p. 55). Building on this scholarship, inside SAYS spaces, students' writing is as precious as any holy manuscript. As demonstrated above, we slow down to contemplate the poem—and in the process, the person who wrote it experiences the transcendent reciprocity of seeing and being seen, hearing and being heard.

CONCLUSION

SAYS strives to create spaces wherein students' lives are the primary text (Watson, 2017). To fully appreciate this idea, Winterson (2011) teaches, "A tough life needs a tough language—and that is what poetry is. That is what literature offers—a language powerful enough to say how it is. It isn't a hiding place. It is a finding place" (p. 40). Similarly, in his best-selling memoir *Heavy*, Laymon (2018) provides an astonishing account of his childhood, coming of age in Mississippi, and his relationship with words, white folks, and the generations of Black women that raised him. He shares, "I realized telling the truth was way different from finding the truth, and finding the truth had everything to do with revisiting and rearranging words. Revisiting and rearranging words didn't only require vocabulary; it required will, and maybe courage" (p. 86).

Many of us, like Winterson and Laymon, have survival stories: experiences and intergenerational traumas that eat us alive and torment us into a form of nihilism and numbness. This is not all of who we are, but pain can be paralyzing. Often it is that which we bury that weighs us down. In a quest to be free from our own suffering, poetry can become a cathartic emancipatory exercise. The poet Khalil Gibran echoed something similar in his own poetry: "Out of suffering have emerged the strongest souls; the most massive characters are seared with scars" (1923; n.p.).

SAYS wants participants to experience that they are already whole and holy—we are all just trying to put the pieces back together. Spiritually grounded practices (e.g., Palmer, 1993) such as this move us from piecemeal to peace, from disconnection to connection. Offering a fresh way of doing *lectio divina* is a form of resistance to an educational system wrought with inequities and dehumanizing pedagogies.

The divine text is us. And through rituals of awakening, learning becomes the soul of social change.

As demonstrated in the case of SAYS, classrooms are sites for opening up in community, growing, and healing. But far too often, we expect students to compartmentalize tasks and engage with curriculum that is irrelevant to their lives. Holistic strategies, on the other hand, activate and actualize a sense of full belonging. As a transformative praxis, *lectio divina*, as sacred reading process, paired together with spoken word poetry, provides a platform for divine discovery, contemplative creativity, and emerging imaginations. This form of pedagogy aligns art, science, and soul—nurturing an awakening that brings us closer to ourselves and each other.

ESSENTIAL IDEAS TO CONSIDER

- We are the authors of our own lives and agents of change.
- Poets have served a sacred role as storyteller, teacher, and communicator. In many societies, these lyrical artists are heralded as cultural keepers and movement makers.
- Spoken word performance poetry, in particular, is deeply emotional, provocative, and public. It embraces full-bodied knowing.

- Speaking truth to power is at the core of the art of spoken word poetry and performance. It isn't always pretty, yet seeks truth as a matter of justice.
- Through rituals of awakening, such as dynamically combining *lectio divina* and spoken word performance poetry, learning becomes a praxis of personal transformation and beloved community.
- Between what is and what could be, there is poetry.

REFERENCES

Akom, A. A. (2009). Critical hip hop pedagogy as a form of liberatory praxis. *Equity & Excellence in Education*, *42*(1), 52–66.
Brecht, B. (2015). Brecht on art and politics. London, UK: Bloomsbury Publishing.
Clark, C. (2004). *After Mecca: Women poets and the Black Arts Movement.* New Brunswick, NJ: Rutgers University Press.
Dalton, J. E. (2018). Embracing a contemplative life: Art and teaching as a journey of transformation. In J. E. Dalton, K. Byrnes, & E. Dorman (Eds.), *The teaching self: Contemplative practices and pedagogy in pre-service teacher education* (pp. 13–25). Lanham, MD: Rowman & Littlefield.
Emdin, C. (2016). *For white folks who teach in the hood . . . and the rest of y'all too: Reality pedagogy and urban education.* Boston, MA: Beacon Press.
Ensley, C. (2015). *The fifth element: Social justice pedagogy through spoken word poetry.* New York, NY: SUNY Press.
Enriquez, G. (2016). Reader response and embodied performance: Body-poems as performative response and performativity. In G. Enriquez, E. Johnson, S. Kontovourki, & C. A. Mallozzi (Eds.), *Literacies, learning, and the body: Putting theory and research into pedagogical practice* (pp. 41–56). New York, NY: Routledge.
Faulkner, S. L. (2009). Research/poetry: Exploring poet's conceptualizations of craft, practice, and good and effective poetry. *Educational Insights*, *13*(3), 1–23.
Fisher, M. (2005). From the coffee house to the school house: The promise and potential of spoken word poetry in school contexts. *English Education*, *37*(2), 115–31.
Fisher, M. (2007). *Writing in rhythm: Spoken word poetry in urban classrooms.* New York, NY: Teachers College Press.
Freire, P. (1993). *Pedagogy of the oppressed.* (M. B. Ramos, Trans.). New York, NY: Continuum. (Original work published 1970.)
Gibran, K. (1923). *The prophet.* New York, NY: Knopf.
Greene, M. (2009). In search of a critical pedagogy. In A. Darder, M. Baltodano, & R. D. Torres (Eds.), *The critical pedagogy reader* (pp. 97–112). New York, NY: Routledge.
Haddix, M. (2013). Visionary response: Listening "face-to-face" and "eye-to-eye": Seeing and believing Black girls and women in educational practice and research. *Counterpoints*, *454*, 191–99.
Hall, M. P., O'Hare, A., Santavicca, N., & Jones, L. F. (2015). The power of deep reading and mindful literacy: An innovative approach in contemporary education. *Innovacion Educativa*, *15*(67), 49–60.
Hill, M. L. (2010). Talking beyond schools of education. In Jennifer A. Sandlin, Brian D. Schultz, & Jake Burdick (Eds.), *Handbook of public pedagogy* (pp. 592–603). New York, NY: Routledge.
Hope, J. K. (2018). Poetic justice: Bay area Afro-Asian women's activism through verse. In Herbert G. Ruffin II & Dwayne A. Mack (Eds.), *Freedom's racial frontier: African Americans in the twentieth-century west* (pp. 128–45). Norman, OK: University of Oklahoma Press.
Jocson, K. (2008). *Youth poets: Empowering literacies in and out of schools.* New York, NY: Peter Lang.
Laymon, K. (2018). *Heavy: An American memoir.* New York, NY: Scribner.

Lorde, A. (1984). Poetry is not a luxury. In *Sister Outsider* (pp. 36–39). Trumansburg, NY: Crossing Press.
Love, B. (2012). *Hip hop's li'l sistas speak: Negotiating identities and politics in the new south*. New York, NY: Peter Lang.
Merton, T. (1968). *Conjectures of a guilty bystander*. New York, NY: Doubleday Image.
Moon, K. (2014, 12 November). Valves, salves, and blueprints: Poetry as artivism. *Teachers & Writers*. Retrieved from http://teachersandwritersmagazine.org/valves-salves-and-blueprintspoetry-and-artivism-355. htm.
Palmer, P. J. (1993). *To know as we are known: Education as a spiritual journey*. San Francisco, CA: Harper.
Patel, L. (2016). *Decolonizing educational research: From ownership to answerability*. New York, NY: Routledge
Rose, T. (1994). *Black noise: Rap music and black culture in contemporary America*. Middletown, CT: Wesleyan University Press.
Sandoval, C., & Latorre, G. (2008). Chicana/o artivism: Judy Baca's digital work with youth of color. In A. Everett (Ed.), *Learning race and ethnicity: Youth and digital media* (pp. 81–108). Cambridge, MA: MIT Press.
Schmidt, K., & Beucher, B. (2018). Embodied literacies and the art of meaning making. *Pedagogies: An International Journal, 13*(2), 119–32.
Shakur, T. (2006). *The rose that grew from concrete*. London: Pocket Books.
Stanton, V., & Tinguely, V. (2001). *Impure—Reinventing the word: The theory, practice, and oral history of "spoken word" in Montreal* (S. de Lobtiniére-Harwood, Trans.). Montreal, QC: Conundrum Press.
Stevenson, B. (2015). *Just mercy: A story of justice and redemption*. New York, NY: Spiegel & Grau.
Watson, V. (2013). Censoring freedom: Community-based professional development and the politics of profanity." *Equity & Excellence in Education, 46*(3), 387–410.
Watson, V. (2016). Literacy is a civil write: The art, science and soul of transformative classrooms. In R. Papa & Eadens, D. M. (Eds.), *Social justice instruction: Empowerment on the chalkboard* (pp. 307–23). (Book Series on Education, Equity and the Economy). New York, NY: Springer.
Watson, V. (2017, winter). Life as primary text: English classrooms as sites for soulful learning. Invited submission for the *Journal of the Assembly for Expanded Perspectives on Learning*, an affiliate of the National Council of Teachers of English. *JAEPL, 22*, 6–18.
Weinstein, S. (2018). *The room is on fire: The history, pedagogy, and practice of youth spoken word poetry*. Albany, NY: State University of New York Press.
Weiss, J., & Herndon, S. (2001). *Brave new voices: The Youth Speaks guide to teaching spoken word poetry*. Portsmouth, NH: Heinemann.
Winterson, J. (2011). *Why be happy when you can be normal*. New York, NY: Grove Press.
Yagelski, R. P. (2009). A thousand writers writing: Seeking change through the radical practice of writing as a way of being. *English Education, 42*(1), 6.

Chapter Nine

The Restorative Power of *Lectio Divina* and the Arts for University Lecturers

Daphne Loads,
University of Edinburgh

Whereas preservice teachers in traditional K–12 educational programs are required to take part in substantial theoretical study and supervised practice, university educators have traditionally received little or no preparation for their teaching roles. To address this gap, many universities now have specialized centers offering in-service workshops, academic programs, team and individual consultations, and facilitated reflection on teaching practice. Collectively, these activities are known as academic (or faculty) development.

There is more to development than the acquisition of technical competence and propositional knowledge. We need university educators who embody integrity, reflectiveness, and compassion in their practice, and such attributes cannot be developed through narrowly instrumental instruction and the straightforward transfer of information. We need development activities that have the potential for transformation.

We can set the stage for transformation by combining elements of the traditional practice of *lectio divina* with arts-enriched methods. A growing body of evidence points to the value of *lectio divina* for university students (see, for example, Keator, 2018), but practices drawing on *lectio divina* are also relevant for university lecturers themselves.

There is a strong tradition of drawing on the processes and sensibilities of the arts in continuing professional development for educators. For example, Black (2002) showed that drawing, metaphor, and conversation allowed teachers access to intuition, values, and feelings and helped them to bring previously unconscious material into awareness. Participants gained knowledge and understanding both of their work contexts and of their own meaning-making processes, so that they were able to make better-informed decisions about their teaching.

Upitis, Smithrim, Garbati, and Ogden (2008) examined the weekly creative sessions of a group of university teachers over five years. Through art making, the participants were able to transcend their everyday work, take care of themselves, deepen and equalize their relationships with colleagues, manage difficult experiences, and have a positive impact on their workplace.

THE IMPOVERISHMENT OF ACADEMIA AND THE FIVE RICHES OF *LECTIO DIVINA*

There is a widespread perception that academic life has become impoverished in recent years. As Palmer and Zajonc (2010) put it, "something essential has gone missing, something that brought coherence and true purpose to our colleges and universities" (p. 73).

The practice of *lectio divina* has the potential to restore some of what has been lost. Five riches in particular can be identified: presence, slowing down, embodied response, trust, and transformation. This fivefold categorization was partly inspired by Hart's (2012) "*Lectio Divina*?" which in turn is a response to Brown's (2008) account of the woodenness of much contemporary Christian worship and his plea for the restoration of imagination and exploration.

In academic practice informed by *lectio divina*, texts are experienced as overflowing with meaningful presence. This presence may not be immediately discernible: It is likely to require a slowing down of our usual reading habits, giving time to reflect and respond. Nor is it discerned through the intellect alone, but through an embodied response that includes sensation and emotion.

The disposition of the reader that is fostered is one of trust: The reader approaches the text with an attitude of openness and an understanding that his or her own judgment of its value is trustworthy. Finally, the act of reading is understood as a path to transformation: The reader, through deep engagement with the text, may be profoundly changed.

NEOLIBERALISM AND PRESENCE

The impoverishment of academic life is, for many commentators, a result of what has come to be called the neoliberal university. This is shorthand for the accusation that the heart has been removed from higher education and replaced by "the market," leaving no room for any other values or guiding principles.

For students this means the commodification of education and their demotion to the status of consumers. For academics it means intense pressure to compete for scarce resources in precarious situations. For academic developers it means disregard for their developmental role and demands for quick fixes and demonstrable results. For everyone, this crude materialism and narrow instrumentalism can lead to a profound sense of emptiness: something important is absent.

Lectio divina, by contrast, is concerned with presence. In the Christian tradition this refers to God; however, within academic development, it is framed within a secular worldview. Here, presence is about meaning and meaning-making: the possibilities that are latent in written texts and the active presence of the reader who brings them to life.

At first glance there may seem to be a clash of values in bringing *lectio divina* into contemporary academic settings. Whereas academic development is largely secular and is considered to be rational and evidence based, *lectio divina* is ancient, spiritual, and mysterious.

Academic colleagues tend to be wary of the introduction of this unfamiliar practice. They may be strongly attached to the idea of the secular university. They are likely to view the history of academia as "a heroic struggle to wrest consciousness and knowledge from the forces of unconsciousness and ignorance" (Dirkx, 1997, p. 79). *Lectio divina*, with its quiet insistence on the extrarational and an acceptance of unknowing, may seem like a capitulation of the Enlightenment: a falling back into darkness.

Moreover, academics' individual histories have followed a journey from wondering child to knowledgeable adult and from layperson to disciplinary expert. They will understandably resent any invitation to relinquish their status and to revert to ways of reading that run counter to their disciplinary training.

To allay participants' concerns, it is necessary to explain the purpose of unfamiliar activities that may at first seem mystifying or even pointless. Tempting as it is to plunge participants into a surprising activity without preamble or preparation, this can be experienced as disrespectful and may be counterproductive. In those situations where it is important for participants to experience a particular activity before discussing it, they are asked to suspend judgment until later, when there will be plenty of time for explanations and analysis.

It is important to offer ideas and activities rather than to impose them. Ground rules are helpful: All participants need to be clear that it is perfectly appropriate to opt out at any time and it is acknowledged that some individuals will find that this particular path to development is not for them. It is, however, important to challenge stereotypical statements such as, "This is all very well for some people, but it doesn't work for scientists!" Experience shows that the lessons of *lectio divina* are valuable for colleagues from a wide range of disciplinary backgrounds. The riches offered by this ancient practice are very much needed in what can be experienced as the impoverished environment of contemporary academia.

In the final section, an example is given of how *lectio divina* can contribute to professional development. Here, the principles behind the practice are outlined.

In small groups university lecturers are invited to read together both literary and nonliterary texts as a starting point for reflection on their teaching practices and teacher identities. The texts studied include not only poems, excerpts from novels, dramas, and short stories, but also extracts from academic papers, policy documents, and other written materials. The depth of engagement comes from the slow pace of reading and the attention paid to the whole experience: emotions, sensations, associations, and memories.

Word by word and line by line, participants are asked to consider what is being said and what it means to them, particularly in relation to their teaching. The process does not necessarily follow the traditional pattern of *lectio*, *meditatio*, *oratio*, and *contemplatio*, but draws on the five riches of *lectio divina* described above: presence, slowing down, embodied response, trust, and transformation.

Jennifer Williams (https://jlwilliamspoetry.co.uk/) is a poet with whom I offer a short workshop to junior academics in the hope that they will leave with new perspectives on teaching, learning, writing, and reading. They begin by reading an abstract from an academic paper that has been rewritten—word for word—backward. The purpose of this is to encourage participants to reflect on the text from a strange new perspective. They often notice subtleties that they had previously missed, and patterns that had not before been visible.

Then another shift of perspective is introduced. Participants are invited to consider words like *butter* and *homesickness* and to identify their opposites, moving on from this strange territory to more familiar academic concepts like *teaching* and *learning* and a corresponding range of potential antonyms. In this way participants experience and work with the presence of meaning in many forms, including ambiguities, paradoxes, associations, and emotions.

INFORMATION, FORMATION, AND TRANSFORMATION

Educators are learners and can be supported to engage in the kinds of learning that are potentially transformative. Transformative learning is said to occur when an individual becomes aware of an assumption that shapes or colors their thinking, and reflects critically on that assumption, identifying possible alternatives (Mezirow, 1997). A profound experience of engaging with a text can prompt or support this process of reassessing assumptions about teaching, learning, and students.

However, a major challenge for academic developers is that hard-pressed colleagues, short of time, often seem to take a reductive approach to their teaching. They demand information about "what works" and reject opportunities for their own formation and transformation as teachers. An overreliance on narrow interpretations of evidence-based practice can lead them to overlook the complex, context-dependent nature of their teaching roles.

They may have a similarly impoverished understanding of teacher development. Too often in busy universities a narrative of constraint drowns out the narrative of growth (O'Meara, Terosky, & Neumann, 2008). The former looks for straightforward solutions to problems such as large class sizes, unfamiliar technology, poor student evaluations, and disruptive organizational restructuring. The latter promotes the development over time of thoughtful, principled practice that takes full account of both teachers' professional judgment and students' agency.

It is arguable whether academics actually take such a reductive approach in their own discipline, and it is clear that they do not apply such principles to other aspects of their life, such as romantic relationships or child-rearing. Nevertheless, they often assume that teaching can be reduced to a series of technical instructions, unaware of Palmer's (1998) wise reminder that "good teaching cannot be reduced to technique; good teaching comes from the identity and integrity of the teacher" (p. 16).

Lectio divina lends itself to gradual growth rather than quick solutions. It teaches acceptance of what Keats (1817) called negative capability, when we are "capable of being in uncertainty, mystery, doubts, without any irritable reaching after fact and reason" (p. 136). But it is also a path to knowledge and understanding, and it is this dialectic between mystery and meaning (Hart, 2012) that is one of its strengths.

In development sessions, participants are invited to encounter both the mystery and the meaning of the texts they read. Any pieces of writing that can tell us something about teaching might be selected. Participants begin by identifying a word or phrase that has particular resonance for them and then try to answer a set of questions, for example:

- What strikes you as surprising or significant about this text/line/word?
- What do you notice about its form?
- What questions does it raise?
- What ambiguities and contradictions are you aware of?
- What resonates with you?

Participants are then invited to make creative connections with their practice:

- How can you relate this to something you already understand about your teaching?
- Is there an important idea here that you can use in your thinking?
- Have you any teaching experience that sheds light on this idea?

In this way we come to appreciate texts not as packages of information, but rather as rich opportunities for personal and professional transformation.

LACK OF TIME AND SLOWING DOWN

One obvious characteristic of contemporary academia is the perceived pace of life. There never seems to be enough time to honor both teaching and research, to reflect with colleagues, to get to know students, to see beyond the next deadline. The slowness of *lectio divina* can act as a restorative, but it is important to remember how difficult it can be for colleagues who are accustomed to frantic busyness to slow down and take the time they need for reading and reflection.

During development workshops, participants are invited to consider metaphors, both fresh and lively examples and those that have become deadened with overuse. For example, we might reflect on the term *woke* as applied to university teachers who are aware of their role in promoting social justice. Are we too tired to be woke? Or has the term itself become a little tired and ironic?

Participants are encouraged to linger longer than usual with ambiguity and uncertainty, by making time for repeated reading and silent contemplation. They are urged to slow down their meaning-making so that they can come to a considered, nuanced understanding of themselves as teachers. For example, they might create a plasticine model representing "embedding" or "innovation" as a way of refreshing their understanding of words that have become stale.

THE DISEMBODIED ACADEMIC AND THE MUNCHERS AND MUMBLERS

There is a long tradition of discomfort with the body in academia that has led to neglect of both the sensual and the emotional dimensions of learning, teaching, and professional development. The myth of the disembodied academic has also hampered acknowledgement of embodied inequalities related to gender, race, disability, and poverty.

Although we may think of monks as disregarding or even despising the body, nevertheless in their practice of *lectio divina* they were known as "munchers and mumblers" (Illich, 1993, p. 54). They fully experienced the sound of the words in their ears and the feel of the words in their mouths. *Lectio divina* allows for a holistic approach to reading that is a healthy antidote to the concept of the academic or student as merely "a brain on a stick" (Lewis, 2006, p. 100).

One way of helping colleagues to reembody their thinking is to encourage them to create artefacts in response to their reading. Brigid Collins (https://www.brigidcollins.co.uk/) is an illustrator, artist, and educator. In her workshops she welcomes participants into a room filled with an abundance of "stuff": paper of all kinds, ribbons, wools, sheets of coppery and silvery metal, printing ink, spools of wire, and paperclips. There are enticing tools and toys including hammers and blocks of print, scissors, knives, and needles as well as paintbrushes and pots of ink and paint. The contrast with the bleakness of many lecture halls and seminar rooms is striking.

Collins facilitates the creation of "poem houses" (Collins & Grisoni, 2012). She gives each participant a brown paper bag that contains fragments of maps, pages torn from old books, photographs, a glue stick, bits of wallpaper. Each bag also contains a small cardboard box. Participants are invited to identify words or phrases from poems that they have been reading closely and that have some resonance for them. They cut these extracts from books, stamp them on metal labels, or print them with wooden blocks using ink pads.

Next they use the cardboard boxes to make houses for their chosen words to dwell in. Academics often refer metaphorically to "grasping ideas," "constructing arguments," and "thinking outside the box." It can come as a relief to them physically to take hold of card, glue, and paper and to make beautiful and intriguing things. Later they spend time in contemplation and discussion of their poem-houses, noticing ambiguities, patterns, and questions and making connections with their identities and practices as educators. As Collins explains, "The combining of poetry and assemblage in these 'Poem House' forms amounts to a conscious attempt to create the conditions in which an 'uncovering' may happen, by means of a process of layered collage and juxtaposed words and images" (Collins, 2019).

SUSPICION AND TRUST

In some academic disciplines, contemporary concern with critique seems to have overshadowed all other ways of reading and responding to texts, leading to an overwhelming atmosphere of suspicion. Felski (2015) describes how the mistrustful reader "advances holding a shield, scanning the horizon for possible assailants, fearful of being tricked or taken in" and in so doing "cuts herself off from a swathe of intellectual and experiential possibility" (p. 12).

Lectio divina can reconnect us with more trusting ways of reading and responding to texts. Not only can the text be appreciated, but the readers can learn to trust their own responses. They can also work collegially, coming to trust each other's feedback. In practice, participants often need reassurance about their capacity to make sound judgments about what is relevant and to dismiss their fears of "hocus-pocus" and naivete relating to *lectio divina*.

Smart and Loads (2017) have written about an activity developed by Smart that she describes as poetic transcription with a twist. Poetic transcription is a term borrowed from arts-based research, in which transcripts of interviews with research participants are distilled into poems by researchers. In this version, adapted for teachers' professional development, Smart invites early career academics to come together to share stories of their experiences of academic life and to work with these stories in a fresh way.

Participants prepare in advance a short written account of a "critical incident" from their recent teaching practice: an experience that has significance for them. Working in silence, in a contemplative mode that contrasts with their usual busyness, group members slowly read and reread each other's writings. From the text of the critical incident, each group member constructs a poem and gives it a title. In order to create the poem, participants can remove words but cannot add them. They must not alter the order of the words in the original piece. Each then reads out his or her poem, and the writer of the original piece is invited to respond, before a group discussion of the experience and what it means for them as teachers.

These group meetings are characterized by a developing sense of trust among early career academics who may be feeling isolated and fearful due to the intense pressures of trying to fit into a new academic post.

LECTIO DIVINA IN ACTION: AN EXAMPLE

Here is an example of how the five riches of *lectio divina* are used in my own development as an educator. It takes the form of an individual response to two short poems: "Tears, Idle Tears" by Alfred Tennyson (1847) and "Virtue" by George Herbert (1633). In the former, the speaker suggests a mood of exquisite regret, showing how in the midst of life we are in death. In the latter, we are brought out into a lovely spring day before being reminded that all of its beauties will perish, since "all must die."

I have known these two pieces for about forty years, and despite this familiarity I continue to read them carefully, line by line and word by word: surely evidence of slowing down? My response to each is intensely embodied. I see the almost painful redness of Herbert's rose, and feel a visceral sense of loss as Tennyson's reddening sails sink below the horizon at sunset.

These poems serve as "teaching texts" for me, but what they have to offer is so much more than mere information. Rather, they shed light on an experience of transformation. Both poems seem to respond to the same implied question, and I feel very keenly the differences between their two responses. In "Virtue" the implied question of "how much?" is answered by "so," and it is this modest word that is illuminated for me as I read. It suggests a rightness: "just so," a precision that requires no external reference.

Tennyson's speaker, by contrast, seems melodramatic. How deep? "Deep as love," then "deep as first love": Presumably the former comparison was inadequate. And then he adds, "and wild with all regret." What can he mean by this? Herbert's "But though the whole world turn to coal," although also extreme, is somehow more believable: It feels steadier in its purpose.

Pondering the differences in mood between the two poems—the one extravagant and the other calmly self-assured, I recognize a profound shift in my own being and understanding. Whereas previously charmed by excesses of emotion and a sense of mystery ("Tears, idle tears, I know not what they mean"), latterly I have become more comfortable with a balance of knowing and not knowing. Over the years, something about my professional and personal identity has taken on the quality of "season'd timber" that "never gives."

That transformation continues to involve placing trust in my capacity for sound judgment. There is always the potential for mistakes. Am I missing an allusion that is obvious to others? Am I reading too much into that line? Are my responses anachronistic? However, even misreadings can be of value. I sometimes mistakenly read "foot" for "root" in "Virtue." This slip adds a vivid touch to the image of a rose, like a person, standing with one foot in the grave. Similarly, I frequently read "slowly glows"—for grows—"a glimmering square": Again the slip seems to intensify my appreciation of the image.

For me, these poems shimmer with presence. As I turn them over in my mind, I see different associations and make different connections. My reflection on these two poems and their implied question—how much?—brings to mind "the measured university" (Peseta, Barrie, & McLean, 2017). That phrase brings together two meanings of *measured* in the neoliberal university: the value of thoughtful, considered action, and the threat of surveillance and performativity.

My own experiences of *lectio divina* enable me to present the practice to participants with authenticity and passion.

CONCLUSION

Academic developers are concerned with helping university lecturers to understand and enhance their teaching and ultimately their students' learning. It is important that this work goes beyond the merely technical and addresses some of the issues that have resulted in the impoverishment of contemporary academic life. Participants are encouraged to read closely and collaboratively, drawing on some of the qualities of *lectio divina*. This enables us to reject narrowly instrumental approaches to professional development and to bring teachers into view in contrast with misguided interpretations of student-centeredness that tend to erase them from the picture.

We claim back literature as a source of wisdom and insight, trusting our responses to poems, novels, and drama and also responding to the literary qualities of nonliterary texts. Importantly, we are able to reintroduce beauty and joy into university teaching that has come to be perceived as bleak and unfulfilling.

ESSENTIAL IDEAS TO CONSIDER

- Academic development is concerned with the understanding and enhancement of university teaching and learning.
- A range of challenges currently facing academic development can be addressed by the practice of *lectio divina* in combination with artwork.
- A personal practice provides a strong base for development work with workshop participants.

REFERENCES

Black, A., 2002. Making sense of what it means to teach: Artful representations as meaning-making tools. *Teacher Development*, 6(1), 75–88.
Brown, D. (2008). *God and mystery: Experience in metaphor and drama*. Oxford: Oxford University Press.
Collins, B. (2019, February 26). Personal communication.
Collins, B., & Grisoni, L. (2012). Sense making through poem houses: An arts-based approach to understanding leadership. *Visual Studies*, 27(1), 35–47.
Dirkx, J. (1997). Nurturing soul in adult learning. *New Directions for Adult and Continuing Education*, 74, 79–88.
Felski, R. (2015). *The limits of critique*. Chicago, IL: University of Chicago Press.
Hart, T. (2012). Lectio divina? In R. MacSwain & T. Worley (Eds.), *Theology, aesthetics and culture: Responses to the work of David Brown* (pp. 226–40). Oxford: Oxford University Press.
Herbert, G. (1874). *The complete works of George Herbert*. Oxford, UK: Pantianos Classics.
Illich, I. (1993). *In the vineyard of the text: A commentary to Hugh St. Victor's didascalicon*. Chicago, IL: University of Chicago Press.
Keator, M. (2018). *Lectio divina as contemplative pedagogy: Re-appropriating monastic practice*. New York, NY: Routledge.
Keats, J. (1817). In H. E. Rollins (Ed.). (1958). *The letters of John Keats*. Cambridge: Cambridge University Press.
Lewis, H. (2006). *Excellence without a soul? Does liberal education have a future?* New York, NY: Public Affairs.
Mezirow, J. (1997). Transformative learning: Theory to practice. *New Directions for Adult and Continuing Education*, 74, 5–12.

O'Meara, K., Terosky, A.L., & Neumann, A. (2008). Faculty careers and work lives: A professional growth perspective. *ASHE Higher Education Report, 34*(3).

Palmer, P. J. (1998). *The courage to teach: Exploring the inner landscape of a teacher's life.* San Francisco, CA: Jossey-Bass.

Palmer, P. J., & Zajonc, J. (2010). *The heart of higher education: A call to renewal: Transforming the academy through collegial conversations.* San Francisco, CA: Jossey-Bass.

Peseta, T., Barrie, S., & McLean, J. (2017). Academic life in the measured university: Pleasures, paradoxes and politics. *Higher Education Research & Development, 36*(3), 453–57.

Smart, F., & Loads, D. (2017). Poetic transcription with a twist: Supporting early career academics through liminal spaces, *International Journal for Academic Development, 22*(2), 134–43.

Tennyson, A. (2006). *The princess.* Los Angeles, CA : The Hard Press.

Upitis, R., Smithrim, K., Garbati, J., & Ogden, H. 2008. The impact of art-making in the university workplace. *International Journal of Education and the Arts, 9*(8), 1–24.

Appendix A

John Keats's poem "To Autumn"

Season of mists and mellow fruitfulness,
Close bosom-friend of the maturing sun;
Conspiring with him how to load and bless
With fruit the vines that round the thatch-eves run;
To bend with apples the moss'd cottage-trees,
And fill all fruit with ripeness to the core;
To swell the gourd, and plump the hazel shells
With a sweet kernel; to set budding more,
And still more, later flowers for the bees,
Until they think warm days will never cease,
For summer has o'er-brimm'd their clammy cells.
Who hath not seen thee oft amid thy store?
Sometimes whoever seeks abroad may find
Thee sitting careless on a granary floor,
Thy hair soft-lifted by the winnowing wind;
Or on a half-reap'd furrow sound asleep,
Drows'd with the fume of poppies, while thy hook
Spares the next swath and all its twined flowers:
And sometimes like a gleaner thou dost keep
Steady thy laden head across a brook;
Or by a cyder-press, with patient look,
Thou watchest the last oozings hours by hours.
Where are the songs of spring? Ay, Where are they?
Think not of them, thou hast thy music too,—
While barred clouds bloom the soft-dying day,
And touch the stubble-plains with rosy hue;
Then in a wailful choir the small gnats mourn
Among the river sallows, borne aloft

Or sinking as the light wind lives or dies;
And full-grown lambs loud bleat from hilly bourn;
Hedge-crickets sing; and now with treble soft
The red-breast whistles from a garden-croft;
And gathering swallows twitter in the skies.

Index

academia, impoverishment of, 100, 107, 108; neoliberalism and, 100–101; Palmer and Zajonc on, 100; time, lack of, and, 104; trust, lack of, and, 105–106
achievement gap. *See* opportunity gap
Adelman, M., 12
anti-oppressive pedagogy, *lectio divina* and, xv, 72; awareness cultivated by, 72, 74, 74–75, 83, 84; Berila on, 73, 74, 74–75, 77, 83; *contemplatio* phase in, 73, 79; embodied learning and, 74–75, 77, 80, 81, 84; emotional literacy facilitated by, 80–81; holistic education and, 74–75; homework and, 79; *lectio* phase in, 72, 77; *meditatio* phase in, 72–73, 77–78, 81, 82; memory and, 81–83; *oratio* phase in, 73, 78, 82; principles of, 73–74; rereading and, 73, 77–78, 80; Sentipensante Pedagogy and, 75, 80, 83; slowing down and, 81–82; social action inspired by, 82–83; student responses and, 79–83; understanding of text deepened by, 79–80, 84
artivism, 90–93
"At This Party" (Hafiz), 41–45
awareness, vii, 4, 27, 46; anti-oppressive pedagogy cultivating, 72, 74, 74–75, 83, 84; contemplative practice deepening, 5–6, 24; *lectio divina*,

ancient monastic practice of, and, 26; Levine on, 74; mindful reading and seeing and, 50; in student responses, 28–29, 31–32, 83; *visio divina* cultivating, xv, 28–29, 30, 31–33, 33; visual art cultivating, 26, 30

banking concept of teaching, 8
Basho, 55
beholding assignment for *visio divina*, 30–33
bell hooks, 46
Benedict (St.), 3, 4
Berila, B.: anti-oppressive pedagogy and, 73, 74, 74–75, 77, 83; embodied learning and, 74, 74–75, 77; social action and, 83
Birkerts, S., 13, 40
Bland, Denisha, 91
Brecht, Bertoldt, 91
Brown, D., 100
Bruner, Jerome, 42

Cage, John, 30
call-and-response, 93, 94
Changing Lives Through Literature (CLTL), 14
Chittister, J., 49
choice of texts and images for *lectio divina*, 51; students making, 56
Clark, C., 91

CLTL. *See* Changing Lives Through Literature
Collins, Brigid, 105
colonization of poetry, 87
community building, xiii–xiv, 13, 54; deep listening and, 39, 41, 42, 45–46; *lectio* phase and, 16; Palmer on, 40; story-to-poem conversion and, xv, 37–41, 42–43, 44–46, 47; transformative learning and, 37–38, 46
Conley, John J., 61, 68
contemplation, viii
contemplatio phase, 5, 27, 50; anti-oppressive pedagogy and, 73, 79; deep reading and, 15–16, 18–20; story-to-poem conversion and, 42; student responses to, 18–20, 27; transcendence in, 19; wisdom and, 18–19; Writing about Yoga and, 61, 66
contemplative practice, 5; awareness deepened by, 5–6, 24; embodied learning and, 9, 23–24; holistic education and, 6, 6–8, 72; interiority and, 6; Palmer on, 12; transformative learning and, 6–8, 24–25, 33; visual art as, 26
contemplative space: Palmer on, 63; Writing about Yoga requiring, 63–64, 64

Dalton, Jane E., 46, 72–73, 90, 92
darshan, *visio divina* and, viii–ix
deep listening: community building and, 39, 41, 42, 45–46; empathy and, 39, 46; story-to-poem conversion and, 37–38, 39, 41, 42, 43–44, 45–46, 46; transformative learning and, 39
deep reading, *lectio divina* and, 13–14, 40; *contemplatio* phase and, 15–16, 18–20; hyperconnectivity impacting, 12; interiority and, 13; *lectio* phase and, 14, 16–17; *meditatio* phase and, 15, 17; neuroscience on, 13; *oratio* phase and, 15, 18; student responses and, 16–20
democracy, humanities and, xiii
Dewey, John: social integration and, 7; visual art and, 24–25

embodied learning, xiii, xv, 2, 8; anti-oppressive pedagogy and, 74–75, 77, 80, 81, 84; Berila on, 74, 74–75, 77; contemplative practice and, 9, 23–24; poem houses and, 105; SAYS and, 88–89; spoken word performance poetry and, 88–89, 95, 96; story-to-poem conversion and, 47; university lecturers, *lectio divina* for, and, 104–105; *visio divina* and, 30. *See also* Writing about Yoga
emotional intelligence, 25; memory and, 25; neuroscience on, 25
emotional literacy, anti-oppressive pedagogy facilitating, 80–81
empathy, 8, 12, 20, 21; deep listening and, 39, 46; as democratizing, xiii; story-to-poem conversion fostering, 40, 45, 45–46, 46, 46–47

faithfulness, 4
fast food, vii
Faulkner, S. L., 91
Felski, R., 105–106
Fowler, Charles, 25
Franklin, M. A., 26
Freire, P., 89; banking concept of teaching and, 8; storytelling and, 43

Garbati, J., 100
Gibran, Khalil, 96
Goleman, Daniel, 25
Greene, M., 8, 87

Haddix, M., 88
Hafiz, 41–45
Hall, M. P., xiv
Hamma, R. M., 40
Hart, Tobin, 33; interiority and, 6; *lectio divina* categorization by, 100
Herbert, George, 106–107
holistic education, 8–9, 9; anti-oppressive pedagogy as, 74–75; contemplative practice and, 6, 6–8, 72; hooks on, 46; Lichtmann on, 6; Miller, J. P., on, 7, 38; Miller, R., on, 7; Palmer and Zajonc on, 2, 8; social media counteracted by, 37; spoken word performance poetry and, 96; story-to-poem conversion and, 38;

UNESCO goals for, 38; Writing about Yoga as, 69
homework in anti-oppressive pedagogy, 79
Hope, J. K., 91
Hughes, H. J., 56
humanities, democracy and, xiii
humanizing education, 21; *lectio divina* as, 11–12, 20, 21; Zajonc on, 11, 12
hyperconnectivity, deep reading impact on, 12

imaginal mindfulness, viii
insight. *See* wisdom
interiority, 53; contemplative practice and, 6; deep reading and, 13; Hart on, 6

Johnson, M., 23

Kabat-Zinn, Jon, xiv
Kaivalya, Alanna, 64
Katha Upanishad, 62
Keator, Mary, 13
Keats, John, xv, 14–20, 103, 111–112

Lakoff, G., 23
Lantieri, L., 25
Lao-tsu, 54
Latorre, G., 90
Laymon, K., 95
lectio divina, ancient monastic practice of, xiv, 1, 3, 4, 9, 26; awareness and, 26; Benedict and, 3, 4; choosing texts for, 51; faithfulness and, 4; as prayer, 3; recitation, listening to, and, 3–4
lectio divina, curricular adaptation of. *See contemplatio* phase; *lectio* phase; *meditatio* phase; *oratio* phase; *specific topics*
lectio phase, 5, 14, 50; anti-oppressive pedagogy and, 72, 77; community building and, 16; deep reading and, 14, 16–17; story-to-poem conversion and, 41; student responses to, 16–17, 27; transformative learning and, 27; visual art and, 27; Writing about Yoga and, 61, 64–65; Zajonc on, 27
leisure, gift of, 59
Levine, Peter, 74
Lewis, H., xiii, 37

Lichtmann, M.: holistic education and, 6; *lectio divina* described by, 4, 16
Lorde, Audre, 89

Macedo, D., 43
McAdams, D. P., 42
meditatio phase, 5, 50; anti-oppressive pedagogy and, 72–73, 77–78, 81, 82; deep reading and, 15, 17; memory in, 17; story-to-poem conversion and, 41; student responses to, 17, 27; visual art and, 27; Writing about Yoga and, 61, 65
memorization, 52; Quenon on, 51
memory: anti-oppressive pedagogy and, 81–83; emotional intelligence and, 25; *meditatio* phase and, 17; *oratio* phase and, 18
Merton, Thomas, 52, 55; wholeness and, 23
Mezirow, Jack, 7, 38, 39, 46
Miller, B., 56
Miller, J. P., 7, 38
Miller, R., 7
mind-body separation: social media and, 37; standardized education and, xiii
mindful reading and seeing, 50
Morson, G. S., 65
Moule, Jean, 76
Musil, C. M., xiii

nature, *visio divina* in, 53
neoliberalism, 100–101
Neruda, Pablo, 53
neuroscience: deep reading and, 13; emotional intelligence and, 25
Nhat Hanh, Thich, 46
Nouwen, H., 63
Nussbaum, M. C., xiii

Ogden, H., 100
opportunity gap, race and, 71
oratio phase, 5, 50; anti-oppressive pedagogy and, 73, 78, 82; deep reading and, 15, 18; memory in, 18; slowing down and, 18; story-to-poem conversion and, 42; student responses to, 18, 27, 65–66; visual art and, 27; Writing about Yoga and, 61, 65–66

O'Sullivan, E., 24

Palmer, Parker, 103; academia, impoverishment of, and, 100; community building and, 40; contemplative practice and, 12; contemplative space and, 63; deep reading and, 13; holistic education and, 2, 8; wholeness and, 23
pausing, *lectio divina* enabling, 92–93
Pennington, M. B., 4
Plato, 7
poem houses, 105
poetic transcription, 106
poetry, 96; "At This Party," 41–45; Brecht on, 91; colonization of, 87; for the people, 89; "Tears, Idle Tears," 106–107; "To Autumn," xv, 14–20, 111–112; university lecturers, *lectio divina* for, and, 105, 106, 106–107; "Virtue," 106–107. *See also* spoken word performance poetry; story-to-poem conversion
prayer, 3
presence, university lecturers and, 100–102
public schools, US, race in, 71

Quenon, Paul: leisure and, 59; memorization and, 51

race: opportunity gap and, 71; public schools, US, and, 71
recitation, 51; listening to, 3–4. *See also lectio* phase; *oratio* phase
Rendón, L. I., 75
rereading, 50, 52, 58; anti-oppressive pedagogy and, 73, 77–78, 80
Rich, K. R., 43
Rilke, Rainer Maria, 58
rituals of awakening, 88, 96, 97
Roberts, J. L., 30
Rodriguez, L. F., 40
Rousseau, Jean-Jacques, 7
Rumi, 20, 55

Sacramento Area Youth Speaks (SAYS), 88–89, 93–96
Sandoval, C., 90
Sarton, M., 52

SAYS. *See* Sacramento Area Youth Speaks
Scribner, Megan, 2, 8
self-acceptance, Writing about Yoga teaching, 67, 68
Sentipensante Pedagogy, 75, 80, 83
Shakur, Tupac Amaru, 91–92
Sher, G., 51
slowing down, vii, 20, 40, 58; anti-oppressive pedagogy and, 81–82; *oratio* phase and, 18; pausing as, 92–93; spoken word performance poetry and, 88, 92–93; university lecturers, *lectio divina* for, and, 102, 104; *visio divina* and, 30–33
Smart, F., 106
Smithrim, K., 100
social action: anti-oppressive pedagogy inspiring, 82–83; Berila on, 83
social integration, Dewey on, 7
social justice education, xv. *See also* anti-oppressive pedagogy
social media, 41; mind-body separation and, 37
spoken word performance poetry, *lectio divina* and, xv, 88; artivism and, 90–93; call-and-response and, 93, 94; embodied learning and, 88–89, 95, 96; holistic education and, 96; live audience as public for, 90; rituals of awakening and, 88, 96, 97; SAYS and, 88–89, 93–96; slowing down and, 88, 92–93; students lives as primary text in, 95–96; transformative learning and, 92, 97; vulnerability, radical, and, 90, 93, 95; as worldwide phenomenon, 89–90
standardized education, mind-body separation in, xiii
Stevenson, Bryan, 95
storytelling, 43–44; Freire on, 43
story-to-poem conversion, *lectio divina* and: community building through, xv, 37–41, 42–43, 44–46, 47; *contemplatio* phase and, 42; deep listening and, 37–38, 39, 41, 42, 43–44, 45–46, 46; embodied learning and, 47; empathy fostered by, 40, 45, 45–46, 46, 46–47; holistic education and, 38; *lectio* phase and, 41; *meditatio* phase and, 41; *oratio*

phase and, 42; sharing step of, 44–45; storytelling step of, 43–44; transformative learning and, xv, 38–46; writing the poem step of, 44
stress, reduction of, 32–33
student responses, 20, 53–56, 58; anti-oppressive pedagogy and, 79–83; awareness in, 28–29, 31–32, 83; *contemplatio* phase and, 18–20, 27; deep reading and, 16–20; difficulties expressed in, 29, 32; *lectio* phase and, 16–17, 27; *meditatio* phase and, 17, 27; *oratio* phase and, 18, 27, 65–66; *visio divina* and, 31–33; visual art and, 28, 28–29, 29; Writing about Yoga and, 62, 64, 65–66, 66–69

Tao Te Ching (Lao-tsu), 54
"Tears, Idle Tears" (Tennyson), 106–107
Tennyson, Alfred, 106–107
time, lack of, in academia, 104
Tishman, S., 31
"To Autumn" (Keats), xv, 14–20, 111–112
transcendence, *contemplatio* phase and, 19
transformative learning, xiii, xiv, xvi, 8, 9; assumptions questioned in, 102; community building through, 37–38, 46; contemplative practice and, 6–8, 24–25, 33; deep listening and, 39; Greene on, 8; *lectio* phase and, 27; Mezirow on, 7, 38, 39, 46; social media counteracted by, 37; spoken word performance poetry and, 92, 97; story-to-poem conversion as, xv, 38–46; transmission versus, 24; university lecturers, *lectio divina* for, and, 102–104; visual art and, 24–25; wholeness and, 2
transmission, transformation versus, 24
trust: academia, impoverishment of, and, 105–106; university lecturers, *lectio divina* for, and, 106

UNESCO holistic education goals, 38
university lecturers, *lectio divina* for, 99–100, 106–107, 108; academia, impoverishment of, and, 100–101, 104, 105–106, 107, 108; embodied learning and, 104–105; poem houses, 105; poetic transcription, 106; presence and, 100–102; resistance to, 101, 103; slowing down and, 102, 104; transformative learning and, 102–104; trust and, 106
Upitis, R., 100

Van der Kooj, Arjuna, 64
"Virtue" (Herbert), 106–107
visio divina, 30; awareness cultivated by, xv, 28–29, 30, 31–33, 33; beholding assignment for, 30–33; choosing images for, 51; darshan and, viii–ix; embodied learning and, 30; in nature, 53; slowing down and, 30–33; student responses and, 31–33
visual art, *lectio divina* and: awareness cultivated by, 26, 30; as contemplative practice, 26; Dewey on, 24–25; *lectio* phase and, 27; *meditatio* phase and, 27; *oratio* phase and, 27; student responses and, 28, 28–29, 29; transformative learning and, 24–25
vulnerability, radical, 90, 93, 95

Waxler, R. P., xiv, 42
wholeness, 4, 11, 20, 21, 34; Merton on, 23; Palmer on, 23; religious roots of, 23; transformative learning and, 2. *See also* holistic education
William of St. Thierry, 51
Williams, Jennifer, 102
Winterson, J., 95
wisdom: *contemplatio* phase and, 18–19; day-to-day application of, viii; Writing about Yoga and, 68
Wolf, M., 41
Writing about Yoga, xv, 61; beginning of class in, 62; body impacted by, 67; *contemplatio* phase in, 61, 66; contemplative space for, 63–64, 64; heart impacted by, 68; holistic education and, 69; *Katha Upanishad* in, 62; *lectio* phase in, 61, 64–65; *meditatio* phase in, 61, 65; mind impacted by, 67; *oratio* phase in, 61, 65–66; self-acceptance and, 67, 68; soul impacted by, 68; student responses to, 62, 64, 65–66, 66–69; wisdom and, 68

Zajonc, Arthur, 27; academia, impoverishment of, and, 100; holistic education and, 2, 8; humanizing education and, 11, 12; *lectio* phase and, 27

Ziegler, Joanna, 30–31

About the Editors

Jane E. Dalton is an artist and associate professor of art education at the University of North Carolina at Charlotte. Her research interests include contemplative practices and pedagogy, social-emotional and transformative learning in classrooms using the arts. She is author for and coeditor of the three-book series Contemplative Practices, Pedagogy, and Research in Education, published in 2018 by Rowman & Littlefield, and coauthor of *The Compassionate Classroom: Lessons that Nurture Empathy and Wisdom* (2004). She can be found online at www.janedalton.com.

Maureen P. Hall is professor at the University of Massachusetts Dartmouth, where she focuses on the intersections between and among mindfulness, literacies, and social-emotional learning (SEL). She has published more than seventeen articles in peer-reviewed journals, and her books include *Transforming Literacy* (2011) with Robert Waxler and *Writing from the Inside* (2019).

Catherine E. Hoyser is professor of English and director of women's and gender studies at the University of Saint Joseph. She teaches postcolonial literature with a focus on forced migration, immigration, and refugee status, British cultural studies, detective fiction, gender studies, and feminist theories. Her publications include *Woman: An Affirmation* and *Tom Robbins: A Critical Companion* as well as scholarly articles. She is also a published poet.

About the Contributors

Elizabeth Hope Dorman is associate professor of teacher education at Fort Lewis College, a public liberal arts college in Durango, Colorado, where she teaches graduate and undergraduate students in secondary, P–12, elementary education, and teacher leadership programs. Her scholarship focuses on the integration and effects of mindfulness and contemplative pedagogies on teacher development of social-emotional competence, particularly in diverse contexts and courses that address multicultural perspectives, social justice education, and equity issues. She is author for and coeditor of the three-book series Contemplative Practices, Pedagogy, and Research in Education, published in 2018 by Rowman & Littlefield.

Libby Falk Jones, professor emerita of English at Berea College, has published essays on contemplative writing and seeing as well as creative nonfiction and poems in numerous journals and anthologies. She has made presentations and led workshops on contemplative pedagogies at Association for Contemplative Mind in Higher Education, Conference on College Composition and Communication and American Educational Research Association, as well as at various colleges and universities.

Mary Keator, PhD, is an assistant professor in the English Department at Westfield State University in Massachusetts and author of *Lectio Divina as Contemplative Pedagogy* (2018); "A Three-Tiered Monastic Approach to Intersubjective Dialogue for Application within Higher Education," in *Catalyzing the Field: Second-Person Approaches to Contemplative Learning and Inquiry* (2019); "Reclaiming the Deep Reading Brain in the Digital Age"; and "The Gift of the Sublime: A Contemplative Reading of Mary Shelley's *Frankenstein*."

Daphne Loads is an academic developer in the Institute for Academic Development at the University of Edinburgh, UK. She studied English literature, life and thought at Cambridge and has professional qualifications in social work, counseling, and higher education teaching and course design. Her research interests include arts-enriched professional development and academic identities. She balances her academic work by traveling with her partner and tending her garden.

Vajra Watson is director of research and policy for equity at the University of California, Davis and founder of Sacramento Area Youth Speaks (SAYS). As a scholar-activist, she seeks innovative ways to align people and systems that advance social justice. Her books include *Learning to Liberate* (2012) and *Transformative Schooling* (2018).

www.ingramcontent.com/pod-product-compliance
Lightning Source LLC
Chambersburg PA
CBHW021846220426
43663CB00005B/425